Lecture Notes in Computer Science   13567

More information about this series at https://link.springer.com/bookseries/558

Hien V. Nguyen · Sharon X. Huang ·
Yuan Xue (Eds.)

Data Augmentation, Labelling, and Imperfections

Second MICCAI Workshop, DALI 2022
Held in Conjunction with MICCAI 2022
Singapore, September 22, 2022
Proceedings

Editors
Hien V. Nguyen
University of Houston
Houston, TX, USA

Sharon X. Huang 🆔
Pennsylvania State University
University Park, PA, USA

Yuan Xue 🆔
Johns Hopkins University
Baltimore, MD, USA

ISSN 0302-9743 ISSN 1611-3349 (electronic)
Lecture Notes in Computer Science
ISBN 978-3-031-17026-3 ISBN 978-3-031-17027-0 (eBook)
https://doi.org/10.1007/978-3-031-17027-0

This Springer imprint is published by the registered company Springer Nature Switzerland AG
The registered company address is: Gewerbestrasse 11, 6330 Cham, Switzerland

Preface

This volume contains the proceedings of the 2nd International Workshop on Data Augmentation, Labeling, and Imperfections (DALI 2022), which was held on September 22, 2022, in conjunction with the 25th International Conference on Medical Image Computing and Computer Assisted Intervention (MICCAI 2022). While this is the second workshop under the "DALI" name, the first DALI workshop (DALI 2021) was the result of a joining of forces between previous MICCAI workshops on Large Scale Annotation of Biomedical Data and Expert Label Synthesis (LABELS 2016–2020) and on Medical Image Learning with Less Labels and Imperfect Data (MIL3ID 2019–2020).

Obtaining the huge amounts of labeled data that modern image analysis methods require is especially challenging in the medical imaging domain. Medical imaging data is heterogeneous and constantly evolving, and expert annotations can be prohibitively expensive and highly variable. Hard clinical outcomes such as survival are exciting targets for prediction but can be exceptionally difficult to collect. These challenges are especially acute in rare conditions, some of which stand to benefit the most from medical image analysis research. In light of this, DALI aims to bring together researchers in the MICCAI community who are interested in the rigorous study of medical data as it relates to machine learning systems.

The DALI 2022 workshop received 24 paper submissions from authors all over the world, from which 22 papers were sent for peer review. Each paper was reviewed by three peer-experts and, in the end, 12 high-quality papers were selected for publication. The workshop was a single-track, full-day workshop consisting of presentations for each of these 12 papers, as well as longer-form invited talks from Ehsan Adeli of Stanford University, Daniel Rückert of the Technical University of Munich, Yefeng Zheng of Tencent Jarvis Lab, Zhen Li from the Chinese University of Hong Kong (Shenzhen), and Vishal M. Patel from Johns Hopkins University.

No scientific program would be successful without a monumental effort on the part of its peer reviewers. We are deeply grateful to the 24 scientists who volunteered a substantial amount of their time to provide valuable feedback to the authors and to help our editorial team make final decisions. The high quality of the scientific program of DALI 2022 was due to the authors who submitted excellent, original contributions. We would like to thank all the authors for submitting their valuable contributions to the workshop. We would also like to thank Rulai Inc., Uzer Inc., and United Imaging Intelligence for their generous financial support of the DALI workshop.

August 2022

Hien V. Nguyen
Sharon X. Huang
Yuan Xue

Organization

Organizing Committee

Hien V. Nguyen	University of Houston, USA
Sharon X. Huang	Pennsylvania State University, USA
Yuan Xue	Johns Hopkins University, USA

Advisory Board

Dimitris N. Metaxas	Rutgers University, USA
Stephen Wong	Houston Methodist Hospital, USA
Nicholas Heller	University of Minnesota, USA
S. Kevin Zhou	University of Science and Technology of China, China
Jia Wu	MD Anderson Cancer Center, USA
Ehsan Adeli	Stanford University, USA

Program Committee

Amogh S. Adishesha	Pennsylvania State University, USA
Ti Bai	UT Southwestern Medical Center, USA
Weidong Cai	University of Sydney, Australia
Nicha Dvornek	Yale University, USA
Yubo Fan	Vanderbilt University, USA
Christoph M. Friedrich	University of Applied Sciences and Arts Dortmund, Germany
Michael Goetz	German Cancer Research Center, Germany
Nicholas Heller	University of Minnesota, USA
Mahdi Hosseini	University of New Brunswick, Canada
Edward Kim	Drexel University, USA
Xingyu Li	University of Alberta, Canada
Xiao Liang	UT Southwestern Medical Center, USA
Gilbert Lim	National University of Singapore, Singapore
Luyang Luo	Chinese University of Hong Kong, China
Haomiao Ni	Pennsylvania State University, USA
Hui Qu	Adobe Inc., USA
Emanuele Trucco	University of Dundee, UK
Zuhui Wang	Stony Brook University, USA

Contents

x   Contents

Image Synthesis-Based Late Stage Cancer Augmentation and Semi-supervised Segmentation for MRI Rectal Cancer Staging

Saeko Sasuga[1]([⊠]), Akira Kudo[1], Yoshiro Kitamura[1], Satoshi Iizuka[2],
Edgar Simo-Serra[3], Atsushi Hamabe[4], Masayuki Ishii[4], and Ichiro Takemasa[4]

[1] Imaging Technology Center, Fujifilm Corporation, Tokyo, Japan
saeko.sasuga@fujifilm.com
[2] Center for Artificial Intelligence Research, University of Tsukuba, Ibaraki, Japan
[3] Department of Computer Science and Engineering,
Waseda University, Tokyo, Japan
[4] Department of Surgery, Surgical Oncology and Science,
Sapporo Medical University, Hokkaido, Japan

Abstract. Rectal cancer is one of the most common diseases and a major cause of mortality. For deciding rectal cancer treatment plans, T-staging is important. However, evaluating the index from preoperative MRI images requires high radiologists' skill and experience. Therefore, the aim of this study is to segment the mesorectum, rectum, and rectal cancer region so that the system can predict T-stage from segmentation results.

Generally, shortage of large and diverse dataset and high quality annotation are known to be the bottlenecks in computer aided diagnostics development. Regarding rectal cancer, advanced cancer images are very rare, and per-pixel annotation requires high radiologists' skill and time. Therefore, it is not feasible to collect comprehensive disease patterns in a training dataset. To tackle this, we propose two kinds of approaches of image synthesis-based late stage cancer augmentation and semi-supervised learning which is designed for T-stage prediction. In the image synthesis data augmentation approach, we generated advanced cancer images from labels. The real cancer labels were deformed to resemble advanced cancer labels by artificial cancer progress simulation. Next, we introduce a T-staging loss which enables us to train segmentation models from per-image T-stage labels. The loss works to keep inclusion/invasion relationships between rectum and cancer region consistent to the ground truth T-stage. The verification tests show that the proposed method obtains the best sensitivity (0.76) and specificity (0.80) in distinguishing between over T3 stage and underT2. In the ablation studies, our semi-supervised learning approach with the T-staging loss improved specificity by 0.13. Adding the image synthesis-based data augmentation improved

---

Supplementary Information The online version contains supplementary material available at https://doi.org/10.1007/978-3-031-17027-0_1.

H. V. Nguyen et al. (Eds.): DALI 2022, LNCS 13567, pp. 1–10, 2022.
https://doi.org/10.1007/978-3-031-17027-0_1

the DICE score of invasion cancer area by 0.08 from baseline. We expect that this rectal cancer staging AI can help doctors to diagnose cancer staging accurately.

Keywords: Rectal cancer · Segmentation · T stage discrimination · Semi-supervised learning · Image synthesis

1   Introduction

T-staging is an index for assessing the spread of primary tumors into nearby tissues. Regarding rectal cancer which is a common disease and a major cause of mortality. Magnetic resonance imaging (MRI) is commonly used for the assessment of T2/T3/T4 staging. In the clinical research [3,16] , it has become clear that invasion depth from rectum and margin between cancer and mesorectum are directly related to the prognosis of rectal cancer, and those indexes are also important for deciding rectal cancer treatment plan. However, evaluating T-staging from preoperative MRI images requires high radiologists' skill and experience. In [13], the T3 staging sensitivity and specificity for experienced gastrointestinal radiologists is 96% and 74%, while for a general radiologist is 75% and 46%, respectively. Since those numbers are not sufficiently high, computer aided diagnosis (CAD) systems for assisting T-staging were proposed in the previous studies [10].

This paper deals with two difficulties in building such CAD systems. First one is that preparing per-pixel annotation requires high radiologists' skill and time cost. Second one is that advanced cancer cases are very rare. Due to these difficulties, it is almost impossible to collect large scale high quality training dataset. To tackle these problems, we propose semi-supervised learning and image synthesis-based late stage cancer augmentation. Here we pick up related works, then summarize contributions of this work.

Cancer Segmentation and T-staging. Since the U-net [14] was proposed, segmentation tasks have achieved remarkable results. Regarding tumor segmentation tasks from MR images, it is reported that segmentation accuracy reached human expert level [5,7,9]. However, not so many researches have been done on automatic T-staging. One research [4] tried to segment tumor, inner wall, and outer wall to visualize cancer invasion, but it did not evaluate T-staging accuracy. Kim et al. [10] proposed a method for classifying T-stage from preoperative rectal cancer MRI, but their method was not able to visualize the basis of the decision. To the best of our knowledge, there was no previous study that simultaneously evaluate both cancer segmentation and T-staging accuracy.

Data Augmentation. Supervised learning methods rely on a large and diverse training dataset to achieve high performance. Data augmentation is commonly known as an effective way to compensate limited amount of training data [15]. Recently, generation-based approach using generative adversarial

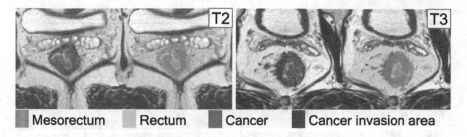

Mesorectum   Rectum   Cancer   Cancer invasion area

Fig. 1. T-stage classification algorithm using multi-label relationship. Yellow arrows point cancer area extends beyond the rectum area and this case is staged with T3. (Color figure online)

networks (GANs) [6] have been proposed. One such method is label-to-image translation. Abhishek et al. [1] used label-to-image translation method to generate skin cancer 2D images for data augmentation and showed improvement in segmentation accuracy. However, this method has limitations that the generated data follow training data distribution. It is difficult to create images that are rarely included in training data.

We summarize the contributions of this work as follows:

1. This is an early work which develops and evaluates a CAD system that can do both rectal cancer segmentation and T-staging with a clinical dataset.
2. We propose a semi-supervised learning using a novel T-staging loss. The T-staging loss enables us to train a segmentation model with not only per-pixel labels but per-image T-stage labels.
3. We propose a label-to-image translation based severe cancer augmentation. This approach can generate rare data that is out of training dataset distribution by deforming cancer label into the shape of a progressive cancer.

2 Methodology

We model the rectal cancer T-staging problem as a multi-class multi-label segmentation of mesorectum, rectum, and rectal cancer as shown in Fig. 1. The algorithm predicts T-stage following to the segmentation results. When the cancer area is not in contact with the contour of the rectum area, the case is classified as under T2 stage. On the other hand, when the cancer area crosses over the rectum area, the case is classified as over T3 stage. This rule exactly follows the T-staging rules of tumor invasion into the area of the rectum. In this section, we explain a semi-supervised approach with a novel loss function named T-staging loss in Sect. 2.1. Then, we explain image synthesis-based late stage cancer augmentation in Sect. 2.2.

2.1 Semi Supervised Learning with T-staging Loss

The proposed semi supervised learning architecture is shown in Fig. 2. We use a 3D variant of U-net that we train to perform a segmentation task. The last

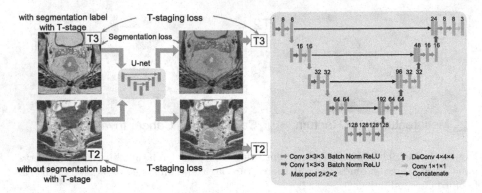

Fig. 2. Frameworks of our semi-supervised learning and the architecture of segmentation network. In the training phase, images with and without segmentation labels are inputted to the U-net. Training data with only T-stage ground truth are used for calculating T-staging loss which works as to maximize correspondence between ground truth and prediction T-stage.

three channels of the network are the probabilities of mesorectum, rectum and rectal cancer areas. T-staging results are calculated based on the binarized segmentation results. In the training phase, 3D MR images with ground-truth segmentation labels or just only ground truth T-stage are inputted to the network. The loss function consists of a segmentation loss and the proposed T-staging loss; $Loss_{SEG} + \lambda \times Loss_{STG}$, where λ is a parameter used to balance the two terms. We used a standard Dice loss [11] for $Loss_{SEG}$. The T-staging loss which for accurate staging purposes is defined as follows:

$$Loss_{STG} = -\mu \log \frac{p_{STG}{}^{g_{STG}}}{(1 - p_{STG})^{(g_{STG}-1)}} + \frac{\sum_{i=1}^{N} p_{invT2i} + \alpha}{\sum_{i=1}^{N} p_{invT2i} + \sum_{i=1}^{N} p_{invT3i} + \alpha}. \quad (1)$$

where,

$$p_{STG} = \max(p_{cancer,i} \times (1 - p_{rectum,i})). \quad (2)$$

$$g_{STG} = \begin{cases} 1 & \text{if ground truth T stage is over T3} \\ 0 & \text{otherwise} \end{cases}. \quad (3)$$

$$p_{invT2} = p_{cancer} \times (1 - p_{rectum}) \times (1 - g_{staging}). \quad (4)$$

$$p_{invT3} = p_{cancer} \times (1 - p_{rectum}) \times g_{staging}. \quad (5)$$

N is the number of voxels. p_{cancer} and p_{rectum} represent the probability maps of the rectal cancer and rectum, respectively. $p_{staging}$ indicates the probability of the predicted staging. It takes a high value when there is any voxel simultaneously having low rectum probability and high cancer probability. p_{invT2} and p_{invT3} are probabilities of cancer invasion of each voxel in T2 case and T3 case. This term works to reduce the cancer area outside of the rectum for T2 cases. On the other hand, it works to increase the cancer area outside of the rectum for

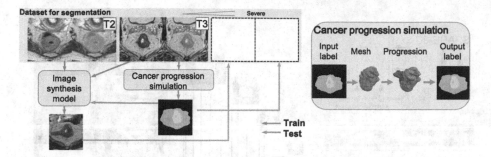

Fig. 3. Overview of severe cancer data syntheses framework. The image synthesis model is trained with real images. On the test phase, cancer labels are modified by simulation. Following the generated labels, image synthesis model generate severe cancer images.

T3 cases. In contrast to $Loss_{SEG}$ is used only for the images with ground-truth segmentation labels. $Loss_{STG}$ can be used for all cases having only ground truth T-staging. So, it works as semi-supervised setting in segmentation.

2.2 Generating Advanced Cancer MRI Image from Labels

Figure 3 is an overview of advanced cancer image synthesis system. In general, GAN can model the underlying distribution of training data. To the contrary, our goal is to generate out-of-distribution data (e.g., we have relatively many early stage cancer, but we want more advanced staged cancer images). Therefore, we first train a label-conditional-GAN model. Then we generate images for data augmentation by inputting various deformed label images. An important point is that the deformation is done by external knowledge which simulate cancer development.

Semantic Image Synthesis. SPADE [12] is known as one of the best architectures for the semantic image synthesis task. However, it is rarely applied on 3D images due to their large computational cost. This is an early work applying SPADE for 3D image synthesis. Overall, we adopt and extended the basic framework of SPADE from 2D to 3D. As shown in Fig. 4, we simply introduce a SPADE-3D block in each scale of the generator instead of residual-SPADE block which was proposed in the original paper to save computational cost.

We found that the more the kinds of input label classes, the more generated images give realistic looking and anatomically consistent. For that reason, in addition to cancer, we also used rectum, mesorectum, bladder, prostate and pelvis classes as the input to the generator. We monitored the training until the generator gives realistically looking images from the given test label images.

Cancer Label Deformation. Advanced stage cancer labels are generated as follows. First, a cancer label was transformed to a 3D mesh model consisting of vertices and faces. Next, the furthest invasion point, infiltration direction vector, and non-deformable part were calculated based on cancer morphology [8].

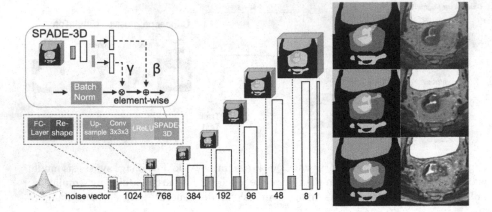

Fig. 4. Overview of the 3D generator architecture. Each normalization layer uses 3D label image to modulate the layer activations. To save computation cost, we removed residual blocks in the original SPADE [12] and introduced a single SPADE-3D block per scale which had enough capacity to generate realistic images.

Fig. 5. Samples of the input labels and generated images. Different images are generated based on the deformed cancer labels.

Then, the 3D mesh model was transformed by constraint shape optimization [2]. Finally, the mesh model was voxelized again. These processes were applied several times for each image, randomly changing a vertex to move and shifting distance. We also mimicked the shape of the cancer infiltrate into vessels or lymph nodes by randomly embedded the tubular or spherical objects to the cancer model. The MR images corresponding to these labels were variously generated by the GAN as shown in Fig. 5 and supplementary movies.

3   Experiments and Results

3.1   Dataset

We curated four types of datasets A–D. The dataset A–C were real MR images acquired from rectal cancer patients. The dataset D was generated by a GAN model which was trained on dataset A. The dataset B was separated from A for a fair comparison, meaning that the dataset D was not generated from testing dataset B. The dataset A, B, and D had per-pixel ground truth labels, and dataset C had only T-stage label. The number of samples in each dataset are provided in Table 1.

MR T2-weighted images were acquired using a 3.0 T (N = 89) or 1.5 T (N = 106) MR scanner. Ground truth segmentation labels were annotated by two surgeons based on the pathological specimens removed by surgeries. Ground truth T-stage labels were labeled based on the pathological diagnosis.

3.2　Implementation Details and Evaluation Metrics

During the training, the Adam optimizer with a learning rate of 0.003 was used. The parameters in the loss function are as follows; $\lambda = 0.1$, $\mu = 0.1, \alpha = 500$. Mini batch consisted of 4 cases with segmentation labels and 2 cases with only T-stage. Experiments were conducted up to 80000 iterations.

Table 1. The dataset specification and usage in this study.

	Patient Num. (T2/T3)	Data type		Usage	
		Image type	Ground truth	Segmentation	Image synthesis
A	69 (22/47)	Real	Label	Train	Train
B	66 (26/40)	Real	Label	Train/Evaluation	Unused
C	60 (29/31)	Real	T-Stage	Train/Evaluation	Unused
D	78 (0/78)	Generated	Label	Train	–

Table 2. The condition of ablation studies.

	Loss function	Dataset
Baseline (DICE loss)	Soft dice	A, B
+Semi supervised	Soft dice + T-staging loss	A, B, C
+Data augmentation	Soft dice + T-staging loss	A, B, C, D

For the evaluation, five-fold cross validation was conducted on dataset B and C. Those evaluation datasets were randomly divided into five subgroups. Four subgroups out of the five and dataset A, and D were used for training the segmentation network. Note that one subgroup in the four subgroups for training was used for validation. We chose the best model according to the DICE score of the validation subgroup, then applied the model to the remaining subgroup. We used two indexes of Dice similarity coefficient in volume [17], and T-staging sensitivity/specificity for evaluation. We calculated T-staging sensitivity as a correctly predicted T3 number divided by the ground truth T3 number. The specificity is a correctly predicted T2 number divided by the ground truth T2 number.

3.3　Results

Ablation studies were conducted to evaluate the efficacies of the proposed methods. We compared three experimental settings shown in Table 2. Each setting corresponds to the baseline (the DICE loss [11]), baseline plus semi-supervised approach, and baseline plus semi-supervised approach and late stage data augmentation.

Table 3. Comparison of DICE score in ablation study.

	Mesorectum	Rectum	Cancer	Invasion area
Baseline (DICE loss)	0.907	0.908	0.642	0.415 [0.330–0.501]
+Semi supervised	**0.910**	0.910	0.669	0.449 [0.380–0.519]
+Data augmentation	0.903	**0.911**	**0.680**	**0.495** [0.413–0.577]

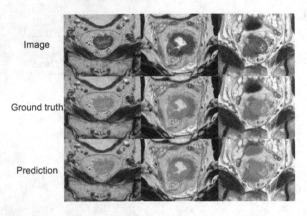

Fig. 6. Example segmentation results. The left column shows T2 cases, the center column is T3 case and the right column is a severe cancer case.

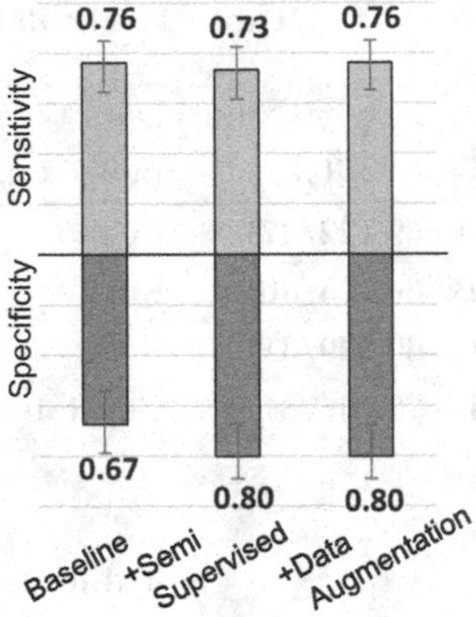

Fig. 7. Comparison of T-staging sensitivity and specificity in ablation study.

We compared the three settings with the Dice coefficients of mesorectum, rectum, cancer and cancer invasion area. Table 3 shows the results of dice coefficient. Figure 6 shows several segmentation results. Both of the semi-supervised and the data augmentation increased the DICE score of cancer area. Especially, they were effective in cancer invasion area. The segmentation results of mesorectum and rectum were not affected by the proposed approach, as is expected. Figure 7 shows results of T-staging accuracy. The proposed method obtains the best sensitivity (0.76) and specificity (0.80), and improved specificity by a margin of 0.13.

4   Discussion

We assumed that the number of available per-pixel training data is small. This often happens at clinical practice. In fact, since rectal cancer is ambiguous on MR images, the surgeons annotated labels with reference to pathological specimens to make reliable ground truth in this research. The T-staging accuracy of the proposed methods was not high enough compared to pathologically proved ground truth. One reason is that T-staging is a hard task for a radiologist too. Another one is that the proposed data augmentation handles only rare shape of the cancer. The future work is generating not only rare shape but rare texture. This study was conducted on data acquired from one site. We are going to validate the algorithm with multi-site data and severe real cancer data.

5   Conclusions

In this paper, we proposed a novel semi-supervised learning method designed for cancer T-staging, and image synthesis-based data augmentation to generate advanced cancer images. Ablation studies showed that the methods improved rectal cancer segmentation and cancer T-staging accuracy. We expect that this cancer segmentation would help doctors diagnose T-staging in clinical practice.

References

1. Abhishek, K., Hamarneh, G.: Mask2Lesion: mask-constrained adversarial skin lesion image synthesis. In: Burgos, N., Gooya, A., Svoboda, D. (eds.) SASHIMI 2019. LNCS, vol. 11827, pp. 71–80. Springer, Cham (2019). https://doi.org/10.1007/978-3-030-32778-1_8
2. Botsch, M., Kobbelt, L.: An intuitive framework for real-time freeform modeling. ACM Trans. Graph. (TOG) **23**(3), 630–634 (2004)
3. Cho, S.H., et al.: Prognostic stratification by extramural depth of tumor invasion of primary rectal cancer based on the radiological society of North America proposal. Am. J. Roentgenol. **202**(6), 1238–1244 (2014)
4. Dolz, J., et al.: Multiregion segmentation of bladder cancer structures in MRI with progressive dilated convolutional networks. Med. Phys. **45**(12), 5482–5493 (2018)
5. Feng, X., Tustison, N.J., Patel, S.H., Meyer, C.H.: Brain tumor segmentation using an ensemble of 3D U-Nets and overall survival prediction using radiomic features. Front. Comput. Neurosci. **14**, 25 (2020)
6. Goodfellow, I., et al.: Generative adversarial nets. In: Advances in Neural Information Processing Systems, vol. 27 (2014)
7. Hodneland, E., et al.: Automated segmentation of endometrial cancer on MR images using deep learning. Sci. Rep. **11**(1), 1–8 (2021)
8. Horvat, N., Carlos Tavares Rocha, C., Clemente Oliveira, B., Petkovska, I., Gollub, M.J.: MRI of rectal cancer: tumor staging, imaging techniques, and management. RadioGraphics **39**(2), 367–387 (2019). pMID: 30768361. https://doi.org/10.1148/rg.2019180114
9. Huang, Y.J., et al.: 3-D RoI-aware U-Net for accurate and efficient colorectal tumor segmentation. IEEE Trans. Cybern. **51**(11), 5397–5408 (2020)
10. Kim, J., et al.: Rectal cancer: toward fully automatic discrimination of T2 and T3 rectal cancers using deep convolutional neural network. Int. J. Imaging Syst. Technol. **29**(3), 247–259 (2019)
11. Milletari, F., Navab, N., Ahmadi, S.A.: V-Net: fully convolutional neural networks for volumetric medical image segmentation. In: 2016 4th International Conference on 3D Vision (3DV), pp. 565–571. IEEE (2016)
12. Park, T., Liu, M.Y., Wang, T.C., Zhu, J.Y.: Semantic image synthesis with spatially-adaptive normalization. In: Proceedings of the IEEE/CVF Conference on Computer Vision and Pattern Recognition, pp. 2337–2346 (2019)

13. Rafaelsen, S.R., Sørensen, T., Jakobsen, A., Bisgaard, C., Lindebjerg, J.: Transrectal ultrasonography and magnetic resonance imaging in the staging of rectal cancer. Effect of experience. Scand. J. Gastroenterol. **43**(4), 440–446 (2008)

14. Ronneberger, O., Fischer, P., Brox, T.: U-Net: convolutional networks for biomedical image segmentation. In: Navab, N., Hornegger, J., Wells, W.M., Frangi, A.F. (eds.) MICCAI 2015. LNCS, vol. 9351, pp. 234–241. Springer, Cham (2015). https://doi.org/10.1007/978-3-319-24574-4_28

15. Shorten, C., Khoshgoftaar, T.M.: A survey on image data augmentation for deep learning. J. Big Data **6**(1), 1–48 (2019)

16. Taylor, F.G., et al.: Preoperative magnetic resonance imaging assessment of circumferential resection margin predicts disease-free survival and local recurrence: 5-year follow-up results of the MERCURY study. J. Clin. Oncol. **32**(1), 34–43 (2014)

17. Zou, K.H., et al.: Statistical validation of image segmentation quality based on a spatial overlap index. Acad. Radiol. **11**(2), 178–189 (2004)

DeepEdit: Deep Editable Learning for Interactive Segmentation of 3D Medical Images

Andres Diaz-Pinto[1,6]($\boxtimes$), Pritesh Mehta[1], Sachidanand Alle[6],
Muhammad Asad[1], Richard Brown[1], Vishwesh Nath[6], Alvin Ihsani[6],
Michela Antonelli[1], Daniel Palkovics[2], Csaba Pinter[3], Ron Alkalay[4],
Steve Pieper[5], Holger R. Roth[6], Daguang Xu[6], Prerna Dogra[6],
Tom Vercauteren[1], Andrew Feng[6], Abood Quraini[6], Sebastien Ourselin[1],
and M. Jorge Cardoso[1]

[1] School of Biomedical Engineering and Imaging Sciences, King's College London,
London, UK
{andres.diaz-pinto,m.jorge.cardoso}@kcl.ac.uk
[2] Department of Periodontology, Semmelweis University, Budapest, Hungary
[3] EBATINCA, S.L. Canary Islands, Spain
[4] Beth Israel Deaconess Medical Center, Boston, MA, USA
[5] Isomics, Inc., Cambridge, MA, USA
[6] NVIDIA Santa Clara, Santa Clara, CA, USA

Abstract. Automatic segmentation of medical images is a key step
for diagnostic and interventional tasks. However, achieving this requires
large amounts of annotated volumes, which can be tedious and time-
consuming task for expert annotators. In this paper, we introduce
DeepEdit, a deep learning-based method for volumetric medical image
annotation, that allows automatic and semi-automatic segmentation, and
click-based refinement. DeepEdit combines the power of two methods: a
non-interactive (i.e. automatic segmentation using nnU-Net, UNET or
UNETR) and an interactive segmentation method (i.e. DeepGrow), into
a single deep learning model. It allows easy integration of uncertainty-
based ranking strategies (i.e. aleatoric and epistemic uncertainty computation) and active learning. We propose and implement a method for
training DeepEdit by using standard training combined with user interaction simulation. Once trained, DeepEdit allows clinicians to quickly
segment their datasets by using the algorithm in auto segmentation
mode or by providing clicks via a user interface (i.e. 3D Slicer, OHIF).
We show the value of DeepEdit through evaluation on the PROSTA-
TEx dataset for prostate/prostatic lesions and the Multi-Atlas Labeling
Beyond the Cranial Vault (BTCV) dataset for abdominal CT segmentation, using state-of-the-art network architectures as baseline for comparison. DeepEdit could reduce the time and effort annotating 3D medical

Supplementary Information The online version contains supplementary material
available at https://doi.org/10.1007/978-3-031-17027-0_2.

H. V. Nguyen et al. (Eds.): DALI 2022, LNCS 13567, pp. 11–21, 2022.
https://doi.org/10.1007/978-3-031-17027-0_2

images compared to DeepGrow alone. Source code is available at https://
github.com/Project-MONAI/MONAILabel.

Keywords: Interactive segmentation · Deep learning · CNNs

1 Introduction

Inspired by the landmark contributions of 2D U-Net [1], 3D U-Net [2], and
V-Net [3], Convolutional Neural Networks (CNN) have become high-performing
methods for automatic segmentation of medical images [4–6]. Medical image segmentation challenges, such as the Medical Segmentation Decathlon (*MSD*) [7],
has helped steer methodological innovations and performance improvements for
CNN-based methods. At the time of writing, one of the first positions on the live
leaderboard[1] for *MSD* is held by the nnU-Net [4], a segmentation pipeline based
on U-Net that automatically configures to any new medical image segmentation
task. More recently, transformer-based [8] networks introduced by Hatamizadeh
et al. (Swin UNETR [9] and UNETR [6]), have further improved on nnUNET's
performance, achieving state-of-the-art performance on the *MSD* segmentation
tasks.

Despite their outstanding performance, automatic segmentation algorithms
have not yet reached the desired level of performance needed for certain clinical applications [10]. In particular, automatic segmentation accuracy can be
impacted by patient variation, acquisition differences, image artifacts [11] and
limited amount of training data. In an attempt to address these challenges,
interactive segmentation methods that accept user guidance to improve segmentation have been proposed [12–15]. Normalized cuts [12], random walks [13],
graph-cuts [14], and geodesics [15] have been proposed for interactive segmentation using bounding-box or scribbles-based user interactions. However, a major
limitation of these classical methods is that they only succeed in addressing sim-
pler segmentation problems where objects have clear structural boundaries, and
require extensive user interaction for more complex segmentation cases containing ambiguity in object boundaries [10].

A number of deep learning-based interactive segmentation methods based
have been proposed for improving the robustness of interactive image segmentation [16,17]. In [16], user foreground and background clicks were converted
into euclidean distance maps, and subsequently learned from as additional input
channels to a CNN. Inspired by the aforementioned studies and other incre-
mental works, interactive methods for medical image segmentation based on
deep learning have been recently proposed [10,18,19]. In [18], a bounding-box
and scribble-based CNN segmentation pipeline was proposed, whereby a user-
provided bounding box is first used to assist the CNN in foreground segmentation. This was followed by image-specific fine-tuning using user-provided scribbles. Due to the inclusion of user interaction within a CNN, this method provided

---

[1] https://decathlon-10.grand-challenge.org/evaluation/challenge/leaderboard/.

greater robustness and accuracy than state-of-the-art for segmenting previously unseen objects, while also using fewer user interactions than existing interactive segmentation methods. In contrast, Sakinis et al. [10] proposed a click-based method, motivated in part by the work of [16]. In their work, Gaussian-smoothed foreground and background clicks were added as input channels to an encoder-decoder CNN. Experiments on multiple-organ segmentation in CT volumes showed that their method delivers 2D segmentations in a fast and reliable manner, generalizes well to unseen structures, and accurately segments organs with few clicks. An alternate method that first performs an automatic CNN segmentation step, followed by an optional refinement through user clicks or scribbles, was proposed by [19]. Their method, named DeepIGeoS, achieved substantially improved performance compared to automatic CNN on 2D placenta and 3D brain tumour segmentation, and higher accuracy with fewer interactions than traditional interactive segmentation methods.

Automatic and semi-automatic segmentation methods are available as part of open-source software packages for medical imaging analysis: ITK-SNAP [20] which offers semi-automatic active contour segmentation [21]; 3D Slicer [22] and MITK [23] offer automatic, boundary-points-based [24]; DeepGrow [10] segmentation through the NVIDIA Clara AI-Assisted Annotation Extension; as well as other classic semi-automatic segmentation methods such as region growing [25] and level sets [26].

We propose DeepEdit, a method that combines an automatic and a semi-automatic approach for 3D medical images into a single deep learning-based model. DeepEdit has three working modes: first, it can be used in click-free inference mode (similar to a regular segmentation network), providing fully-automatic segmentation predictions which can be used as a form of initialisation; second, it allows users to provide clicks to initialise and guide a semi-automatic segmentation model; lastly, given an initial segmentation, DeepEdit can be used to refine and improve the initial prediction by providing editing clicks. DeepEdit training process is similar to the algorithm proposed by Sakinis et al. [10] (Deep-Grow) - Gaussian-smoothed clicks for all labels and background are generated and added as input to the backbone CNN, but removes the minimum-click limitation of DeepGrow. Contrary to DeepGrow, our proposed DeepEdit model allows the prediction of an automatic segmentation-based initialisation without user-provided clicks, which can then be further edited by providing clicks. Lastly, the proposed model can also be used for multi-label segmentation problems, allowing the user to generate/segment all labels simultaneously instead of one label at a time.

The flexibility offered by embedding these three functionalities (auto segmentation, semi-automatic segmentation and label refinement) allows DeepEdit to be integrated into an active learning pipeline. For instance, it could be used in automatic segmentation mode for aleatoric and/or epistemic uncertainty computation to rank unlabeled images (See Fig. 1(b)).

In order to show the performance of DeepEdit, we present applications for single and multiple label segmentation for annotating the datasets: prostate, prostatic lesion, and abdominal organ segmentation.

2 Proposed Method

The DeepEdit architecture is based on a backbone that can be any segmentation network (i.e. UNET, nnU-Net [4], UNETR, SwinUNETR [9]). The main difference resides in how this backbone is trained and the number of channels in the input tensor. For training, the input tensor could be either the image with zeroed tensors (automatic segmentation mode) or the image with tensors representing label and background clicks provided by the user (interactive mode). In Fig. 1, DeepEdit is presented in its training and inference mode.

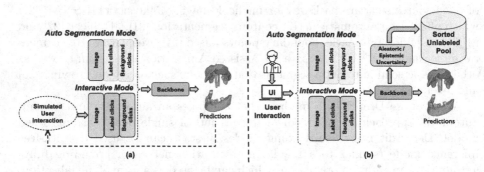

Fig. 1. General schema of the DeepEdit: (a) Training and (b) Inference Mode. DeepEdit training process consists of two modes: the automatic segmentation mode and the interactive mode. Simulated clicks for all labels plus background are added to a backbone network as input channels. Input tensor could be either the image with zero-tensors (automatic segmentation mode) or the image with tensors representing label clicks and background clicks provided by the user (interactive mode).

As shown in Fig. 1, DeepEdit can integrate an active learning strategy in which the trained model is used to rank the unlabelled volumes from the most uncertain to the least uncertain. Every time the expert annotator fetches an image, DeepEdit present the one with more uncertainty, allowing the model to learn from the most challenging cases first.

2.1 User Interaction and Simulated Clicks

Our proposed method embeds three approaches: automatic segmentation, semi-automatic segmentation and interactive segmentation. This means, for some iterations, DeepEdit is trained click-free, and for others is trained as DeepGrow (clicks are simulated and included in the input tensor as extra channels). As

DeepGrow relies on clicks provided by a user or agent, we simulated those following the similar approach presented in Sakinis' work - voxels where clicks are located are set to one and smoothed with a Gaussian filter. This is done for the positive label, if single label task or, in general, for all labels and background.

2.2   Training DeepEdit

As previously mentioned, the training process of the DeepEdit algorithm involves click-free iterations and iterations with simulated clicks. As shown in Fig. 1(a), the input of the network is a concatenation of multiple tensors: the image, a tensor containing clicks simulated for each label and a tensor containing clicks simulated for the background. Our proposed algorithm mixes two types of training loops: a) click-free training iterations - meaning that for some iterations, the tensors representing the labels and background clicks are zeros (training for the automatic segmentation); b) simulated-click based training iterations - where labels and background clicks are simulated and placed in the tensors. We sample from a uniform distribution with probability p to determine which iteration is click-free and which one uses simulated clicks. An additional hyper-parameter, the number of simulated clicks per iteration, is set by the user as a function of the task complexity. These two training loops allow DeepEdit to be used fully automatically, semi-automatic, and as a segmentation refinement approach. We developed all these new transforms for click simulation and mixed training in MONAI [10,27].

3   Experimental Results

In order to demonstrate the flexibility and value of DeepEdit, and the impact of the number of simulated clicks, a set of experiments were performed on the PROSTATEx and Multi Atlas Labeling Beyond The Cranial Vault (BTCV) datasets. We present the impact of the number of clicks in the prostate, prostatic lesion, and abdominal organs (BTCV dataset) segmentation. For both single and multilabel segmentation experiments, we used a learning rate of 1e−4, batch size equal to 1 and Adam optimizer. The following MONAI transforms were used to train and validate DeepEdit: intensity normalization, random flipping (vertically and horizontally), random shift intensity and random rotation.

All our experiments have been implemented using the MONAI Core library [27] (version 0.8.1) and MONAI Label platform (version 0.3.1). All source code for DeepEdit algorithm and Active Learning strategies have been made publicly available and documented at https://github.com/Project-MONAI/ MONAILabel as part of the MONAI Label repository.

3.1   Prostate Segmentation Tasks

DeepEdit applications were built for whole prostate segmentation and prostatic lesion segmentation. Experiments were run using the PROSTATEx Challenge training dataset, [28], hereby referred to as the PROSTATEx dataset. For both single- and multi-label tasks, experiments were conducted to compare the segmentation performance of DeepEdit as the hyperparameter controlling the number of training iterations with zero simulated clicks is varied. We compared DeepEdit on different click-free training iterations: DeepEdit-0 (equivalent to DeepGrow), DeepEdit-0.25 and DeepEdit-0.50, meaning that 0, 25 and 50% of the training iterations were click-free. Ten-fold cross-validation was performed for both tasks. Segmentation quality was assessed using the Dice coefficient. As in [10], segmentation performance at inference time was assessed using simulated clicks instead of user mouse-clicks to objectively assess how segmentation quality improves as clicks are added; segmentation performance was assessed at 0, 1, 5, and 10 simulated inference clicks. The presented results are an average of three repetitions to account for variability in simulated inference click placement.

Whole Prostate Segmentation. The whole prostate segmentation task concerns the segmentation of the prostate on T2-weighted MRI (T2WI). Eleven patients from the PROSTATEx dataset were excluded due to inconsistencies between T2WI and the ground-truth segmentations, leaving a total of 193 patients for use in experiments.

T2WI were pre-processed by resampling to a common resolution of $0.5\,\text{mm} \times 0.5\,\text{mm} \times 3.0\,\text{mm}$, normalization using per-image whitening, and cropping/padding to a common size of $320 \times 320 \times 32$.

A comparison of DeepEdit-0 (equivalent to DeepGrow), DeepEdit-0.25, and DeepEdit-0.5 is shown in Table 1. Furthermore, the distributions of Dice scores are shown in Fig. 2. DeepEdit-0.5 was found to have the highest click-free mean Dice score (0.908), while DeepEdit-0 gave the highest mean Dice scores at 1 to 10 simulated inference clicks.

Table 1. Whole prostate segmentation mean Dice scores ± one standard deviation for the 193 PROSTATEx dataset patients used in the ten-fold cross-validation, for nnU-Net, DeepEdit-0 (equivalent to DeepGrow), DeepEdit-0.25, and DeepEdit-0.5. The highest mean Dice in each column is shown in bold.

Scheme	Model	Number of simulated clicks			
		0	1	5	10
Fully automatic	nnU-Net [4]	**0.910 ± 0.033**	–	–	–
Automatic + interactive editing	DeepEdit-0.25	0.908 ± 0.054	0.912 ± 0.049	0.921 ± 0.041	0.929 ± 0.026
	DeepEdit-0.5	0.908 ± 0.046	0.911 ± 0.044	0.919 ± 0.035	0.926 ± 0.028
Fully interactive	DeepEdit-0 (DeepGrow)	0.907 ± 0.041	**0.915 ± 0.035**	**0.926 ± 0.024**	**0.932 ± 0.020**

Prostatic Lesion Segmentation. The prostatic lesion segmentation task concerns the segmentation of lesions within the prostate using T2WI, apparent diffusion coefficient (ADC) map, and computed high b-value diffusion-weighted MRI (DWI). Since our experiments were conducted using the PROSTATEx dataset, we used the PROSTATEx definition of a lesion, i.e., a prostatic lesion is defined

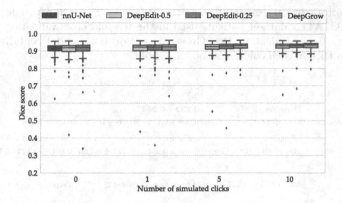

Fig. 2. Whole prostate segmentation: Dice score box plots for the 193 PROSTA-TEx dataset patients used in the ten-fold cross-validation, for DeepEdit-0 (equivalent to DeepGrow), DeepEdit-0.25, and DeepEdit-0.5.

as any area of suspicion attributed to a Prostate Imaging-Reporting and Data System (PI-RADS) score by the expert radiologist (anonymous clinician) who read and reported PROSTATEx dataset cases; all lesions in the PROSTATEx dataset were scored PI-RADS ≥ 2. Four patients from the PROSTATEx dataset were excluded due to not containing contoured lesions in the ground truth (the assessment metrics would have been undefined), leaving a total of 200 patients with a total of 299 lesions for use in experiments.

A b-value, $b = 2000$, was selected for computing high b-value DWI; computed b2000 (Cb2000) DWI were generated using DWI acquired at lower b-values, extrapolated by assuming a monoexponential model for the per-voxel observed signal. ADC map and Cb2000 DWI were registered to T2WI to account for voluntary/involuntary patient movement between acquisitions and differences in resolution. T2WI and Cb2000 DWI were normalised by dividing voxel intensities by the interquartile mean of central gland (CG) voxel intensities [29]; ADC maps were not normalised as they contain a quantitative measurement. T2WI, ADC map, and Cb2000 DWI were resampled to a common resolution of 0.5 mm $\times$ 0.5 mm $\times$ 3 mm. Then, whole prostate masks were used to crop the prostate region on all MR modalities; a margin was applied in each direction to reduce the likelihood of prostate tissue being discarded. Next, a cropping/padding transformation was used to ensure a common spatial size of $256 \times 256 \times 32$.

A comparison of DeepEdit-0 (equivalent to DeepGrow), DeepEdit-0.25, and DeepEdit-0.5 is shown in Table 2. Furthermore, the distributions of Dice scores are shown in Fig. 3. As in the whole prostate segmentation task, DeepEdit-0.5 gave the highest click-free mean Dice score (0.272), while DeepEdit-0 (equivalent to DeepGrow) gave the highest mean Dice scores at 1 to 10 simulated inference clicks.

Table 2. Prostatic lesion segmentation mean Dice scores ± one standard deviation for the 200 PROSTATEx dataset patients used in the ten-fold cross-validation, for nnU-Net, DeepEdit-0 (equivalent to DeepGrow), DeepEdit-0.25, and DeepEdit-0.5. The highest mean Dice in each column is shown in bold.

Scheme	Model	Number of simulated clicks			
		0	1	5	10
Fully automatic	nnU-Net [4]	**0.332 ± 0.254**	–	–	–
Automatic + interactive editing	DeepEdit-0.25	0.268 ± 0.271	0.498 ± 0.174	0.632 ± 0.130	0.697 ± 0.114
	DeepEdit-0.5	0.272 ± 0.266	0.453 ± 0.197	0.592 ± 0.163	0.663 ± 0.145
Fully interactive	DeepEdit-0 (DeepGrow)	0.166 ± 0.254	**0.527 ± 0.166**	**0.670 ± 0.111**	**0.723 ± 0.095**

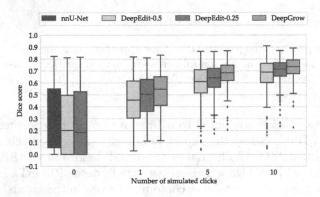

Fig. 3. Prostatic lesion segmentation: Dice score box plots for the 200 PROSTA-TEx dataset patients used in the ten-fold cross-validation, for DeepEdit-0 (equivalent to DeepGrow), DeepEdit-0.25, and DeepEdit-0.5.

3.2   Abdominal Organ Segmentation

A second set of experiments using the UNETR [6] as backbone were performed on the BTCV dataset. For this, we used 23 images for training, 6 for validation, and an image size of $128 \times 128 \times 128$. As the previous analysis, we compared DeepEdit trained with 0% click-free training iterations (equivalent to DeepGrow), 25% click-free training iterations, and 50% click-free training iterations.

In Table 3, we show the obtained results on the validation set for 0, 1, 5, and 10 simulated clicks. As a fair comparison, we trained and validated a UNETR and the DeepEdit using the same images, same transforms and for the same number of epochs (200).

As it is shown in Table 3, any DeepEdit configuration performs slightly better than the UNETR on the validation set when simulated clicks are provided.

Additional qualitative results obtained from DeepEdit are presented in the supplementary material. We show how DeepEdit could also be applied on two additional clinical problems: segmentation of metastatic spines and teeth segmentation for treatment planning in reconstructive periodontal surgery.

Table 3. Dice scores for single and multilabel segmentation on the validation set using the BTCV dataset. For single label we used the spleen organ and multilabel we used spleen, liver, and left and right kidneys. We show the results obtained for 0, 1, 5, and 10 clicks simulated during validation. Highest Dice scores in each column are shown in bold.

Scheme	Model	Single label				Multilabel			
		Number of simulated clicks				Number of simulated clicks			
		0	1	5	10	0	1	5	10
Fully automatic	UNETR	**0.919**	–	–	–	**0.911**	–	–	–
Automatic + interactive editing	DeepEdit-0.25	0.874	**0.902**	0.895	0.895	0.901	0.887	0.900	0.906
	DeepEdit-0.5	0.835	0.850	0.864	0.876	0.875	**0.895**	0.899	0.905
Fully interactive	DeepEdit-0 (DeepGrow)	0.897	0.899	**0.913**	**0.931**	0.892	0.892	**0.914**	**0.926**

4   Conclusion

In this study, we introduce DeepEdit, a method that enables an uncertainty-driven active learning workflow for labelling medical images using a framework that combines deep learning-based automatic segmentation and interactive edits. Compared to previous interactive approaches, DeepEdit can be easily integrated into any 3D medical segmentation pipeline that includes active learning strategies. Using DeepEdit, biologists/clinicians can 1) obtain an automatic segmentation that can later be modified or refined by providing clicks through a user interface (e.g., 3D Slicer, OHIF), or 2) provide clicks to get a segmentation (semi-automatic segmentation). This could significantly reduce the time clinicians/biologists spend on annotating more datasets, which translates in less cost and effort spent on this process.

References

1. Ronneberger, O., Fischer, P., Brox, T.: U-Net: convolutional networks for biomedical image segmentation. In: Navab, N., Hornegger, J., Wells, W.M., Frangi, A.F. (eds.) MICCAI 2015. LNCS, vol. 9351, pp. 234–241. Springer, Cham (2015). https://doi.org/10.1007/978-3-319-24574-4_28
2. Çiçek, Ö., Abdulkadir, A., Lienkamp, S.S., Brox, T., Ronneberger, O.: 3D U-Net: learning dense volumetric segmentation from sparse annotation. In: Ourselin, S., Joskowicz, L., Sabuncu, M.R., Unal, G., Wells, W. (eds.) MICCAI 2016. LNCS, vol. 9901, pp. 424–432. Springer, Cham (2016). https://doi.org/10.1007/978-3-319-46723-8_49
3. Milletari, F., Navab, N., Ahmadi, S.-A.: V-Net: fully convolutional neural networks for volumetric medical image segmentation. In: 3DV (2016)
4. Isensee, F., Jaeger, P.F., Kohl, S.A., Petersen, J., Maier-Hein, K.H.: nnU-Net: a self-configuring method for deep learning-based biomedical image segmentation. Nat. Meth. **18**, 203–211 (2020)
5. He, Y., Yang, D., Roth, H., Zhao, C., Xu, D.: DiNTS: differentiable neural network topology search for 3D medical image segmentation. In: 2021 IEEE/CVF Conference on Computer Vision and Pattern Recognition (CVPR), pp. 5837–5846 (2021)

6. Hatamizadeh, A., et al.: UNETR: transformers for 3D medical image segmentation. In: 2022 IEEE/CVF Winter Conference on Applications of Computer Vision (WACV), pp. 1748–1758 (2022)
7. Antonelli, M., et al.: The medical segmentation decathlon. Nat. Commun. **13**(1), 1–13 (2022)
8. Vaswani, A., et al.: Attention is all you need. In: Proceedings of the 31st International Conference on Neural Information Processing Systems, NIPS 2017, vol. 2017, pp. 6000–6010 (2017)
9. Hatamizadeh, A., Nath, V., Tang, Y., Yang, D., Roth, H.R., Xu, D.: Swin UNETR: swin transformers for semantic segmentation of brain tumors in MRI images. In: Crimi, A., Bakas, S. (eds.) Brainlesion: Glioma, Multiple Sclerosis, Stroke and Traumatic Brain Injuries: 7th International Workshop, BrainLes 2021, Held in Conjunction with MICCAI 2021, Virtual Event, September 27, 2021, Revised Selected Papers, Part I, pp. 272–284. Springer, Cham (2022). https://doi.org/10.1007/978-3-031-08999-2_22
10. Sakinis, T., et al.: Interactive segmentation of medical images through fully convolutional neural networks. arXiv preprint arXiv:1903.08205 (2019)
11. Zhao, F., Xie, X.: An overview of interactive medical image segmentation. Ann. Brit. Mach. Vis. Assoc. **2013**(7), 1–22 (2013)
12. Shi, J., Malik, J.: Normalized cuts and image segmentation. IEEE Trans. Pattern Anal. Mach. Intell. **22**(8), 888–905 (2000)
13. Grady, L., Schiwietz, T., Aharon, S., Westermann, R.: Random walks for interactive organ segmentation in two and three dimensions: implementation and validation. In: Duncan, J.S., Gerig, G. (eds.) MICCAI 2005. LNCS, vol. 3750, pp. 773–780. Springer, Heidelberg (2005). https://doi.org/10.1007/11566489_95
14. Boykov, Y., Funka-Lea, G.: Graph cuts and efficient N-D image segmentation. Int. J. Comput. Vis. **70**(2), 109–131 (2006)
15. Akkus, Z., et al.: Semi-automated segmentation of pre-operative low grade gliomas in magnetic resonance imaging. Cancer Imaging **15**(12), 1–10 (2015)
16. Xu, N., Price, B., Cohen, S., Yang, J., Huang, T.: Deep interactive object selection. In: 2016 IEEE Conference on Computer Vision and Pattern Recognition (CVPR), vol. 1, pp. 373–381 (2016)
17. Agustsson, E., Uijlings, J.R., Ferrari, V.: Interactive full image segmentation by considering all regions jointly. In: 2019 IEEE Conference on Computer Vision and Pattern Recognition (CVPR), vol. 1, pp. 11614–11623 (2019)
18. Wang, G., et al.: Interactive medical image segmentation using deep learning with image-specific fine tuning. IEEE Trans. Med. Imaging **37**(7), 1562–1573 (2018)
19. Wang, G., et al.: DeepIGeoS: a deep interactive geodesic framework for medical image segmentation. IEEE Trans. Pattern Anal. Mach. Intell. **41**(7), 1559–1572 (2019)
20. Yushkevich, P.A., et al.: User-guided 3D active contour segmentation of anatomical structures: significantly improved efficiency and reliability. Neuroimage **31**(3), 1116–1128 (2006). https://doi.org/10.1016/j.neuroimage.2006.01.015
21. Kass, M., Witkin, A., Terzopoulos, D.: Snakes: active contour models. Int. J. Comput. Vis. **1**(4), 321–331 (1988)
22. Fedorov, A., et al.: 3D slicer as an image computing platform for the quantitative imaging network. Magn. Reson. Imaging **30**, 1323–1341 (2012)
23. Nolden, M., et al.: The medical imaging interaction toolkit: challenges and advances: 10 years of open-source development. Int. J. Comput. Assist. Radiol. Surg. **8**(4), 607–620 (2013)

24. Maninis, K.K., Caelles, S., Pont-Tuset, J., Van Gool, L.: Deep extreme cut: from extreme points to object segmentation. In: Proceedings of the IEEE Computer Society Conference on Computer Vision and Pattern Recognition, pp. 616–625 (2018)
25. Adams, R., Bischof, L.: Seeded region growing. IEEE Trans. Pattern Anal. Mach. Intell. **16**(6), 641–647 (1994)
26. Osher, S., Sethian, J.A.: Fronts propagating with curvature-dependent speed: algorithms based on Hamilton-Jacobi formulations. J. Comput. Phys. **79**(1), 12–49 (1988)
27. MONAI Consortium: MONAI: Medical Open Network for AI, March 2020
28. Litjens, G., Debats, O., Barentsz, J., Karssemeijer, N., Huisman, H.: ProstateX Challenge data (2017)
29. Mehta, P., et al.: AutoProstate: towards automated reporting of prostate MRI for prostate cancer assessment using deep learning. Cancers **13**(23), 6138 (2021)

Long-Tailed Classification of Thorax Diseases on Chest X-Ray: A New Benchmark Study

Gregory Holste[1], Song Wang[1], Ziyu Jiang[2], Thomas C. Shen[3], George Shih[4], Ronald M. Summers[3], Yifan Peng[4(✉)], and Zhangyang Wang[1(✉)]

[1] The University of Texas at Austin, Austin, TX, USA
atlaswang@utexas.edu
[2] Texas A&M University, College Station, TX, USA
[3] National Institutes of Health, Bethesda, MD, USA
[4] Weill Cornell Medicine, New York, NY, USA
yip4002@med.cornell.edu

Abstract. Imaging exams, such as chest radiography, will yield a small set of common findings and a much larger set of uncommon findings. While a trained radiologist can learn the visual presentation of rare conditions by studying a few representative examples, teaching a machine to learn from such a "long-tailed" distribution is much more difficult, as standard methods would be easily biased toward the most frequent classes. In this paper, we present a comprehensive benchmark study of the long-tailed learning problem in the specific domain of thorax diseases on chest X-rays. We focus on learning from naturally distributed chest X-ray data, optimizing classification accuracy over not only the common "head" classes, but also the rare yet critical "tail" classes. To accomplish this, we introduce a challenging new long-tailed chest X-ray benchmark to facilitate research on developing long-tailed learning methods for medical image classification. The benchmark consists of two chest X-ray datasets for 19- and 20-way thorax disease classification, containing classes with as many as 53,000 and as few as 7 labeled training images. We evaluate both standard and state-of-the-art long-tailed learning methods on this new benchmark, analyzing which aspects of these methods are most beneficial for long-tailed medical image classification and summarizing insights for future algorithm design. The datasets, trained models, and code are available at https://github.com/VITA-Group/LongTailCXR.

Keywords: Long-tailed learning · Chest X-ray · Class imbalance

---

Supplementary Information The online version contains supplementary material available at https://doi.org/10.1007/978-3-031-17027-0_3.

1 Introduction

Like most diagnostic imaging exams, chest radiography produces a few very common findings, followed by many relatively rare findings [21,32]. Such a "long-tailed" (LT) distribution of outcomes can make it challenging to learn discriminative image features, as standard deep image classification methods will be biased toward the common "head" classes, sacrificing predictive performance on the infrequent "tail" classes [31]. In other settings and modalities, there are a select few examples of LT datasets, such as in dermatology [17] and gastrointestinal imaging [1]; however, the data from Liu et al. [17] are not publicly available, and the *HyperKvasir* dataset [1] – while providing 23 unique class labels with several very rare conditions (<50 labeled examples) – only contains about 10,000 labeled images for classification. Additionally, while many studies offer techniques to combat class imbalance for medical image analysis problems [6,15,19,33], very few methods specifically address the challenges posed by an LT distribution, as there is no freely available benchmark for this purpose.

Only recently have studies begun to use the lens of "LT learning" to describe and improve medical image understanding solutions. For example, Galdran et al. [6] proposed Balanced-MixUp, an extension of the MixUp [29] regularization technique with class-balanced sampling, a common approach in the LT learning literature. Ju et al. [11] grouped rare classes into subsets based on prior knowledge (location, clinical presentation) and used knowledge distillation to train a "teacher" model to enforce the "student" to learn these groupings. Zhang et al. [30] combined a feature "memory" module, resampling of tail classes, and a re-weighted loss function to improve the LT classification of several medical datasets. More broadly, many relevant techniques have been developed in the related fields of imbalanced learning [19,33] and few-shot learning [14,24]. These medical image-specific techniques, plus the wealth of methods from the computer vision literature [2–4,8,9,12,13,16,20,25,28,31], provide a foundation from which the medical deep learning community can develop methods for medical LT classification.

Since no large-scale, publicly available dataset exists for LT medical image classification, we curate a large benchmark (>200,000 labeled images) of two thorax disease classification tasks on chest X-rays. Further, we evaluate state-of-the-art LT learning methods on this data, analyzing which components of existing methods are most applicable to the medical imaging domain.

Our contributions can be summarized as follows:

- We formally introduce the task of long-tailed classification of thorax disease on chest X-rays. The task provides a comprehensive and realistic evaluation of thorax disease classification in clinical practice settings.
- We curate a large-scale benchmark from the existing representative datasets NIH ChestXRay14 [28] and MIMIC-CXR [10]. The benchmark contains five new, more fine-grained pathologies, producing a challenging and severely imbalanced distribution of diseases (Fig. 1). We describe the characteristics of this benchmark and will publicly release the labels.

- We find that the standard cross-entropy loss and augmentation methods such as MixUp fail to adequately classify the rarest "tail" classes. We observe that class-balanced re-weighting improves performance on infrequent classes, and "decoupling" via classifier re-training is the most effective approach for both datasets.

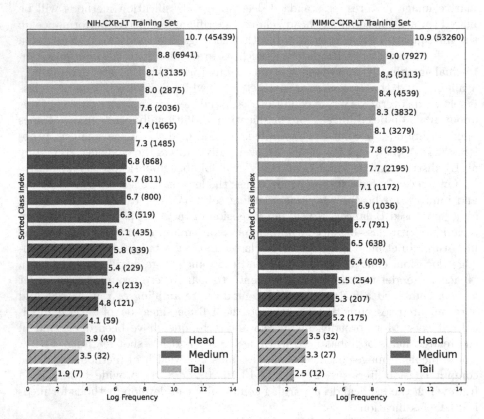

Fig. 1. Long-tailed distribution of thorax disease labels for the proposed NIH-CXR-LT (left) and MIMIC-CXR-LT (right) training datasets. Values by each bar represent log-frequency, while values in parentheses represent raw frequency. Textured bars represent newly added disease labels, which help create naturally long-tailed distributions without the need for artificial subsampling.

2   Long-Tailed Classification of Thorax Diseases

2.1   Task Definition

Disease patterns in chest X-rays are numerous, and their incidence exhibits a long-tailed distribution [21,32]: while a small number of common diseases have sufficient observed cases for large-scale analysis, most diseases are infrequent. Conventional computer vision methods may fail to correctly identify uncommon thorax disease classes due to the extremely imbalanced class distribution [21], introducing a new and clinically valuable LT classification task on chest X-rays. We formulate the LT classification task first by dividing thorax disease classes into "head" (many-shot: >1,000), "medium" (medium-shot: 100–1000, inclusive), and "tail" (few-shot: <100) categories according to their frequency in the training set.

2.2 Dataset Construction

We curate two long-tailed chest X-ray benchmarks, **NIH-CXR-LT** and **MIMIC-CXR-LT**, for NIH ChestXRay14 [26] and MIMIC-CXR [10], respectively. Each study of NIH ChestXRay14 and MIMIC-CXR usually contains one or more chest radiographs and one free-text radiology report. To generate a strongly long-tailed distribution without artificially subsampling, we introduce five new rare disease findings that are text-mined from radiology reports: Calcification of the Aorta, Subcutaneous Emphysema, Tortuous Aorta, Pneumomediastinum, and Pneumoperitoneum. We identify the presence or absence of new disease findings by parsing the text report associated with each study following the method detailed in RadText [23,26].

For this study, we only use frontal-view, single-label images, as most LT methods are developed specifically for multi-class (not multi-label) classification. Following the structure of previous LT benchmark datasets in computer vision, such as ImageNet-LT [18], we split NIH-CXR-LT and MIMIC-CXR-LT into *training*, *validation*, *test*, and *balanced test* sets. Since both datasets contain patients with multiple images, we split them at the patient level to prevent data leakage. Both validation and balanced test sets are small but perfectly balanced, where the balanced test set is a subset of the larger, imbalanced test set. This data split allows for evaluation consistent with the LT literature (via the balanced test set), as well as more traditional evaluation on a large naturally distributed set (via the test set). The resulting splits produce extreme class imbalance, with an *imbalance factor* – the cardinality of the most frequent training class divided by the cardinality of the least frequent training class – of 6,491 for NIH-CXR-LT and 4,438 for MIMIC-CXR-LT. Full detailed statistics and data split for NIH-CXR-LT and MIMIC-CXR-LT can be found in the Supplementary Materials.

NIH-CXR-LT. NIH ChestXRay14 contains over 100,000 chest X-rays labeled with 14 pathologies, plus a "No Findings" class. We construct a single-label, long-tailed version of the NIH ChestXRay14 dataset by introducing five new disease findings described above. The resulting NIH-CXR-LT dataset has 20 classes, including 7 head classes, 10 medium classes, and 3 tail classes. NIH-CXR-LT contains 88,637 images labeled with one of 19 thorax diseases, with 68,058 training and 20,279 test images. The validation and balanced test sets contain 15 and 30 images per class, respectively.

MIMIC-CXR-LT. We construct a single-label, long-tailed version of MIMIC-CXR in a similar manner. MIMIC-CXR is a multi-label classification dataset with over 200,000 chest X-rays labeled with 13 pathologies and a "No Findings" class. The resulting MIMIC-CXR-LT dataset contains 19 classes, of which 10 are head classes, 6 are medium classes, and 3 are tail classes. MIMIC-CXR-LT contains 111,792 images labeled with one of 18 diseases, with 87,493 training images and 23,550 test set images. The validation and balanced test sets contain 15 and 30 images per class, respectively.

Table 1. Long-tailed learning methods selected for benchmarking grouped by type of approach ("R" = Re-balancing, "A" = Augmentation, "O" = Other). "RW" = re-weighted with scikit-learn weights [22], "CB" = re-weighted with class-balanced weights [4].

Method	R	A	O	Method	R	A	O
Softmax (Baseline)				CB LDAM-DRW [2]	✓		
CB Softmax	✓			RW LDAM [2]	✓		
RW Softmax	✓			RW LDAM-DRW [2]	✓		
Focal Loss [16]	✓			MixUp [29]		✓	
CB Focal Loss [16]	✓			Balanced-MixUp [6]	✓	✓	
RW Focal Loss [16]	✓			Decoupling–cRT [12]	✓		✓
LDAM [2]	✓			Decoupling–τ-norm [12]	✓		✓
CB LDAM [2]	✓						

2.3 Methods for Benchmarking

In their survey, Zhang *et al.* group LT learning methods into three main categories: class re-balancing, information augmentation, and module improvement [31]. We simplify this categorization down to re-balancing, augmentation, and others, noting that some sophisticated methods can fall into more than one of these categories. We have summarized our selected methods for benchmarking with their corresponding categorizations in Table 1.

Class re-balancing, arguably the most common approach to LT learning, usually involves *resampling* the data such that it is effectively balanced during training or *re-weighting* a loss function to modulate the importance of classes based on their frequency. Resampling methods include SMOTE [3], which undersamples common classes and oversamples rare classes, and progressively-balanced sampling [12], which interpolates from instance- to class-balanced sampling; recent re-weighting strategies include Focal Loss [16], Label-Distribution-Aware Margin (LDAM) Loss [2], and Influence-Balanced Loss [20]. In addition to the baseline softmax cross-entropy loss function, we consider Focal Loss and LDAM, with optional deferred re-weighting (DRW). For re-weighting strategies, we select the "class-balanced" (CB) approach outlined in [4] and the re-weighting approach implemented by the scikit-learn library [22].

Approaches to "information augmentation" can include customized data augmentation, as well as transfer learning from related data domains. For this category, we choose MixUp [29] and Balanced-MixUp [6]. MixUp is an augmentation technique that linearly mixes pairs of input images and labels according to a Beta distribution, producing a strong regularizing effect. Balanced-MixUp, as explained earlier, is an extension of MixUp that linearly mixes pairs of images and labels, where one image is drawn from a batch of instance-balanced (naturally distributed) data and the other from class-balanced (resampled) data.

Lastly, other popular approaches to LT learning include ensembling, representation learning, classifier design, and decoupled training. For this category, we proceed with two straightforward decoupling methods: classifier re-training (cRT) and τ-normalization. Kang et al. [12] observed that they could achieve state-of-the-art results on several LT learning benchmarks by (1) learning representations from naturally distributed data, then (2) re-training or otherwise calibrating the classification head in order to better discriminate tail classes. After training a model on instance-balanced data, cRT freezes this trained backbone, then re-initializes and re-trains the classifier with class-balanced resampling. Directly using the model learned in step (1), τ-normalization scales each classifier's learned weights by their magnitude raised to the power τ.

2.4   Experiments and Evaluation

We evaluate the list of methods shown in Table 1 on NIH-CXR-LT and MIMIC-CXR-LT. To enable a fair comparison among all methods, we keep the entire training pipeline identical except for the method being applied. Specifically, we train a ResNet50 [7] pretrained on ImageNet [5], using the Adam optimizer with a learning rate of 1×10^{-4}. All models were trained for a maximum of 60 epochs with early-stopping based on overall validation accuracy. For full implementation details, refer to the Supplemental Materials and our code repository: https://github.com/VITA-Group/LongTailCXR.

We present results on both the balanced test set and imbalanced test set for each model and dataset. For the balanced test set, we report head, medium, and tail class accuracy. We additionally include the class-wise average ("overall") accuracy and the group-wise average ("avg") accuracy – namely, the mean of the head, medium, and tail accuracy; we use this metric since we seek a model that performs well across head, medium, and tail classes regardless of how many samples or classes belong to each group. For the imbalanced test set, we report the Macro-F1 score (the unweighted mean of class-wise F1 scores) and the balanced accuracy (the accuracy with samples weighted by inverse class frequency). We choose balanced accuracy since it is resistant to class imbalance, thus necessary since the test set follows the highly imbalanced real-world data distribution.

3   Results and Analysis

For the NIH-CXR-LT dataset, the baseline method fails to adequately classify tail classes, achieving 1.7% accuracy on those three rarest diseases (Table 2). The baseline of softmax cross-entropy loss achieves a group-wise average accuracy of 0.164, but improves to 0.309 and 0.288, respectively, when using class-balanced and scikit-learn weights. Furthermore, we see that re-weighting constantly improves performance, though it is inconsistent which re-weighting method provides more significant gains than others. We also see that DRW can additionally improve performance, as evidenced by the fact that both CB LDAM-DRW and RW LDAM-DRW outperform their counterparts without DRW. We find that cRT decoupling achieves the best performance on both the balanced and imbalanced test sets, reaching 0.369 group-wise average accuracy on the balanced test set and 0.294 balanced accuracy on the test set. Classifier re-training is followed closely by RW LDAM-DRW, reaching 0.362 group-wise average accuracy and 0.294 balanced accuracy.

On MIMIC-CXR-LT, again, the baseline approach almost entirely fails to capture the tail classes, reaching 0.022 tail accuracy and 0.188 group-wise average accuracy (Table 3). Like with the NIH-CXR-LT results, re-weighting is always beneficial; for example, class-balanced re-weighting and scikit-learn re-weighting, respectively, improve focal loss performance from 0.181 to 0.278 and 0.299 group-wise average accuracy. Similarly, DRW brings even further gains to a re-weighted LDAM loss, improving group-wise accuracy by at least 0.05. Classifier re-training again achieves both the highest group-wise average accuracy on the balanced test set and the highest balanced accuracy on the test set by a considerable margin. For both the balanced and imbalanced test sets, the second-best method is a re-weighted LDAM loss with deferred re-weighting – CB LDAM-DRW for the balanced test set and RW LDAM-DRW for the test set.

Summary of Findings. Overall, we see that the standard approach of optimizing softmax cross-entropy with instance-balanced weights fails to adequately capture medium and tail classes for both NIH-CXR-LT and MIMIC-CXR-LT. In contrast to the empirical success of MixUp on many natural image-based problems and Balanced-MixUp on certain medical imaging tasks, we find that MixUp and Balanced-MixUp perform similarly to the baseline for these two tasks; perhaps linearly mixing radiographs destroys valuable high-contrast signal that is necessary for discriminating disease conditions. We see that re-weighting is always beneficial, though which re-weighting method provides larger gains appears to depend on its interaction with the loss function used. We also observe that DRW can provide additional gains to standard re-weighting when used with the LDAM loss. Finally, we see that cRT decoupling was the highest-performing method on both datasets, demonstrating that decoupled training can be a simple and powerful technique for long-tailed disease classification on chest X-rays. We note that reported metrics appear lower than prior work on the original NIH ChestXRay14 and MIMIC-CXR datasets since (1) we use different metrics (primarily accuracy, not area under the receiver operating characteristic curve), (2) we only use single-label images, and (3) the newly added classes are difficult and introduce confusion with the set of original diseases in each dataset.

Table 2. Results on NIH-CXR-LT. Accuracy is reported for the balanced test set ($N = 600$), where "Avg" accuracy is the mean of the head, medium, and tail accuracy. Macro-F1 score (mF1) and balanced accuracy (bAcc) are used to evaluate performance on the imbalanced test set ($N = 20,279$). The best and second-best results for a given metric are, respectively, bolded and underlined.

Method	Balanced test set					Test set	
	Overall	Head	Medium	Tail	Avg	mF1	bAcc
Softmax	0.175	0.419	0.056	0.017	0.164	0.131	0.115
CB Softmax	0.333	0.295	0.415	0.217	0.309	0.177	0.269
RW Softmax	0.300	0.248	0.359	0.258	0.288	0.116	0.26
Focal Loss	0.160	0.362	0.056	0.042	0.153	0.142	0.122
CB Focal Loss	0.303	0.371	0.333	0.117	0.274	0.157	0.232
RW Focal Loss	0.255	0.286	0.293	0.117	0.232	0.090	0.197
LDAM	0.232	0.410	0.133	0.142	0.228	0.173	0.178
CB LDAM	0.295	0.357	0.285	0.208	0.284	0.161	0.235
CB LDAM-DRW	0.377	0.476	0.356	0.250	0.361	0.172	0.281
RW LDAM	0.353	0.305	0.419	0.292	0.338	0.111	0.279
RW LDAM-DRW	0.370	0.410	0.367	0.308	<u>0.362</u>	0.127	<u>0.289</u>
MixUp	0.170	0.419	0.044	0.017	0.160	0.132	0.118
Balanced-MixUp	0.213	0.443	0.081	0.108	0.211	0.167	0.155
Decoupling–cRT	0.380	0.433	0.374	0.300	**0.369**	0.138	**0.294**
Decoupling–τ-norm	0.280	0.457	0.230	0.083	0.257	0.144	0.214

Table 3. Results on MIMIC-CXR-LT. Accuracy is reported for the balanced test set ($N = 570$), where "Avg" accuracy is the mean of head, medium, and tail accuracy. Macro-F1 score (mF1) and balanced accuracy (bAcc) are used to evaluate performance on the imbalanced test set ($N = 23,550$). The best and second-best results for a given metric are, respectively, bolded and underlined.

Method	Balanced test set					Test set	
	Overall	Head	Medium	Tail	Avg	mF1	bAcc
Softmax	0.281	0.503	0.039	0.022	0.188	0.183	0.169
CB Softmax	0.347	0.493	0.167	0.222	0.294	0.186	0.227
RW Softmax	0.314	0.473	0.139	0.133	0.249	0.163	0.211
Focal Loss	0.268	0.477	0.044	0.022	0.181	0.182	0.172
CB Focal Loss	0.288	0.373	0.117	0.344	0.278	0.136	0.191
RW Focal Loss	0.335	0.403	0.283	0.211	0.299	0.144	0.239
LDAM	0.261	0.497	0.000	0.000	0.166	0.172	0.165
CB LDAM	0.330	0.467	0.161	0.211	0.280	0.161	0.225
CB LDAM-DRW	0.379	0.520	0.156	0.356	<u>0.344</u>	0.197	0.267
RW LDAM	0.335	0.437	0.250	0.167	0.284	0.149	0.243
RW LDAM-DRW	0.365	0.447	0.256	0.311	0.338	0.177	<u>0.275</u>
MixUp	0.291	0.543	0.011	0.011	0.189	0.182	0.176
Balanced-MixUp	0.267	0.480	0.039	0.011	0.177	0.176	0.168
Decoupling–cRT	0.412	0.490	0.306	0.367	**0.387**	0.170	**0.296**
Decoupling–τ-norm	0.337	0.520	0.167	0.067	0.251	0.178	0.230

4   Discussion and Conclusion

In summary, we have conducted the first comprehensive study of long-tailed learning methods for disease classification from chest X-rays. We publicly release all code, models, and data to encourage the development of long-tailed learning methods for medical image classification. While we adopted the standard practice of using ImageNet pretrained weights, this limited the list of candidate long-tailed learning methods we could use. For example, certain LT methods that use specialized architectures [25,27] or explore self-supervised learning [9,19] on other datasets are not compatible with ImageNet pretraining. Future work will explore various pretraining options, combating long-tailed data with a different weight initialization. Lastly, future work will also involve adapting multi-label long-tailed learning methods to these datasets, acknowledging the clinical reality that patients often present with multiple pathologies at once.

Acknowledgments. This material is based upon work supported by the Intramural Research Programs of the National Institutes of Health Clinical Center, National Library of Medicine under Award No. 4R00LM013001, and National Science Foundation under Grant No. 2145640.

References

1. Borgli, H., et al.: HyperKvasir, a comprehensive multi-class image and video dataset for gastrointestinal endoscopy. Sci. Data **7**(1), 1–14 (2020)
2. Cao, K., Wei, C., Gaidon, A., Aréchiga, N., Ma, T.: Learning imbalanced datasets with label-distribution-aware margin loss. In: Advances in Neural Information Processing Systems, NeurIPS, pp. 1565–1576 (2019)
3. Chawla, N.V., Bowyer, K.W., Hall, L.O., Kegelmeyer, W.P.: SMOTE: synthetic minority over-sampling technique. J. Artif. Intell. Res. **16**, 321–357 (2002)
4. Cui, Y., Jia, M., Lin, T., Song, Y., Belongie, S.J.: Class-balanced loss based on effective number of samples. In: IEEE Conference on Computer Vision and Pattern Recognition, CVPR, pp. 9268–9277 (2019)
5. Deng, J., Dong, W., Socher, R., Li, L.J., Li, K., Fei-Fei, L.: ImageNet: a large-scale hierarchical image database. In: 2009 IEEE Conference on Computer Vision and Pattern Recognition, pp. 248–255 (2009)
6. Galdran, A., Carneiro, G., González Ballester, M.A.: Balanced-MixUp for highly imbalanced medical image classification. In: de Bruijne, M., et al. (eds.) MICCAI 2021. LNCS, vol. 12905, pp. 323–333. Springer, Cham (2021). https://doi.org/10.1007/978-3-030-87240-3_31
7. He, K., Zhang, X., Ren, S., Sun, J.: Deep residual learning for image recognition. In: Proceedings of the IEEE Conference on Computer Vision and Pattern Recognition, CVPR, pp. 770–778 (2016)
8. Huang, C., Li, Y., Loy, C.C., Tang, X.: Learning deep representation for imbalanced classification. In: Proceedings of the IEEE Conference on Computer Vision and Pattern Recognition, CVPR, pp. 5375–5384 (2016)
9. Jiang, Z., Chen, T., Mortazavi, B.J., Wang, Z.: Self-damaging contrastive learning. In: International Conference on Machine Learning, ICLR, pp. 4927–4939 (2021)

10. Johnson, A.E., et al.: MIMIC-CXR, a de-identified publicly available database of chest radiographs with free-text reports. Sci. Data **6**, 317 (2019)
11. Ju, L., et al.: Relational subsets knowledge distillation for long-tailed retinal diseases recognition. In: de Bruijne, M., et al. (eds.) MICCAI 2021. LNCS, vol. 12908, pp. 3–12. Springer, Cham (2021). https://doi.org/10.1007/978-3-030-87237-3_1
12. Kang, B., et al.: Decoupling representation and classifier for long-tailed recognition. In: International Conference on Learning Representations, ICLR (2020)
13. Kini, G.R., Paraskevas, O., Oymak, S., Thrampoulidis, C.: Label-imbalanced and group-sensitive classification under overparameterization. In: Advances in Neural Information Processing Systems, NeurIPS 34 (2021)
14. Li, X., Yu, L., Jin, Y., Fu, C.-W., Xing, L., Heng, P.-A.: Difficulty-aware meta-learning for rare disease diagnosis. In: Martel, A.L., et al. (eds.) MICCAI 2020. LNCS, vol. 12261, pp. 357–366. Springer, Cham (2020). https://doi.org/10.1007/978-3-030-59710-8_35
15. Lin, C., Wu, H., Wen, Z., Qin, J.: Automated malaria cells detection from blood smears under severe class imbalance via importance-aware balanced group softmax. In: de Bruijne, M., et al. (eds.) MICCAI 2021. LNCS, vol. 12908, pp. 455–465. Springer, Cham (2021). https://doi.org/10.1007/978-3-030-87237-3_44
16. Lin, T., Goyal, P., Girshick, R.B., He, K., Dollár, P.: Focal loss for dense object detection. In: IEEE International Conference on Computer Vision, ICCV (2017)
17. Liu, Y., et al.: A deep learning system for differential diagnosis of skin diseases. Nat. Med. **26**(6), 900–908 (2020)
18. Liu, Z., Miao, Z., Zhan, X., Wang, J., Gong, B., Yu, S.X.: Large-scale long-tailed recognition in an open world. In: IEEE Conference on Computer Vision and Pattern Recognition, CVPR (2019)
19. Marrakchi, Y., Makansi, O., Brox, T.: Fighting class imbalance with contrastive learning. In: de Bruijne, M., et al. (eds.) MICCAI 2021. LNCS, vol. 12903, pp. 466–476. Springer, Cham (2021). https://doi.org/10.1007/978-3-030-87199-4_44
20. Park, S., Lim, J., Jeon, Y., Choi, J.Y.: Influence-balanced loss for imbalanced visual classification. In: Proceedings of the IEEE/CVF International Conference on Computer Vision, ICCV, pp. 735–744 (2021)
21. Paul, A., et al.: Generalized zero-shot chest x-ray diagnosis through trait-guided multi-view semantic embedding with self-training. IEEE Trans. Med. Imaging **40**(10), 2642–2655 (2021). https://doi.org/10.1109/TMI.2021.3054817
22. Pedregosa, F., et al.: Scikit-learn: machine learning in Python. J. Mach. Learn. Res. **12**, 2825–2830 (2011)
23. Peng, Y., Wang, X., Lu, L., Bagheri, M., Summers, R.M., Lu, Z.: NegBio: a high-performance tool for negation and uncertainty detection in radiology reports. AMIA Summits Transl. Sci. Proc. **2018**, 188–196 (2018)
24. Quellec, G., Lamard, M., Conze, P., Massin, P., Cochener, B.: Automatic detection of rare pathologies in fundus photographs using few-shot learning. Medical Image Anal. **61**, 101660 (2020)
25. Shu, J., et al.: Meta-weight-net: learning an explicit mapping for sample weighting. In: Advances in Neural Information Processing Systems, NeurIPS 32 (2019)
26. Wang, X., Peng, Y., Lu, L., Lu, Z., Bagheri, M., Summers, R.M.: ChestX-Ray8: hospital-scale chest x-ray database and benchmarks on weakly-supervised classification and localization of common thorax diseases. In: IEEE Conference on Computer Vision and Pattern Recognition, CVPR, pp. 3462–3471 (2017)
27. Wang, X., Lian, L., Miao, Z., Liu, Z., Yu, S.: Long-tailed recognition by routing diverse distribution-aware experts. In: International Conference on Learning Representations, ICLR (2020)

28. Wang, Y.X., Ramanan, D., Hebert, M.: Learning to model the tail. In: Advances in Neural Information Processing Systems, NeurIPS 30 (2017)
29. Zhang, H., Cisse, M., Dauphin, Y.N., Lopez-Paz, D.: mixup: beyond empirical risk minimization. In: International Conference on Learning Representations (2018)
30. Zhang, R., et al.: MBNM: multi-branch network based on memory features for long-tailed medical image recognition. Comput. Meth. Program. Biomed. **212**, 106448 (2021)
31. Zhang, Y., Kang, B., Hooi, B., Yan, S., Feng, J.: Deep long-tailed learning: a survey. arXiv preprint arXiv:2110.04596 (2021)
32. Zhou, S.K., et al.: A review of deep learning in medical imaging: imaging traits, technology trends, case studies with progress highlights, and future promises. Proc. IEEE **109**(5), 820–838 (2021)
33. Zhuang, J., Cai, J., Wang, R., Zhang, J., Zheng, W.: CARE: class attention to regions of lesion for classification on imbalanced data. In: International Conference on Medical Imaging with Deep Learning, MIDL. Proceedings of Machine Learning Research, vol. 102, pp. 588–597. PMLR (2019)

Lesser of Two Evils Improves Learning in the Context of Cortical Thickness Estimation Models - Choose Wisely

Filip Rusak[1,2(✉)], Rodrigo Santa Cruz[2], Elliot Smith[3], Jurgen Fripp[2], Clinton Fookes[1], Pierrick Bourgeat[2], and Andrew P. Bradley[1]

[1] Queensland University of Technology, Brisbane, QLD, Australia
[2] CSIRO, Herston, QLD, Australia
filip.rusak@csiro.au
[3] Maxwell Plus, Brisbane, QLD, Australia

Abstract. Cortical thickness (CTh) is an important biomarker commonly used in clinical studies for a range of neurodegenerative and neurological conditions. In such studies, CTh estimation software packages are employed to estimate CTh from T1-weighted (T1-w) brain MRI scans. Since commonly used software packages (e.g. FreeSurfer) are time-consuming, the fast-inference Machine Learning (ML) CTh estimation solutions have gained much popularity. Recently, several ML regression-based solutions offering morphological properties (CTh, volume and curvature) estimation have emerged but typically achieved lower accuracy compared to mainstream alternatives. One of the reasons for such performance of the ML-based CTh estimation models is the inaccurate automatic labels typically used for their training. In this paper, we investigate the impact of automatic labels selection on the performance of the current state-of-the-art ML regression-based CTh estimation method - HerstonNet. We train two models on pairs of brain MRIs and FreeSurfer/DL+DiReCT automatic CTh measurements to investigate the benefits of using DL+DiReCT instead of, the more frequently used, FreeSurfer CTh measurements on the learning capability of a modified version of HerstonNet. Then, we evaluate the performance of the two trained models on three test sets with scans coming from four publicly available datasets. We show that HerstonNet trained on DL+DiReCT labels overall achieves a 13.3% higher Intraclass Correlation Coefficient (ICC) on a test set composed of ADNI and AIBL scans, 19.4% on OASIS-3 and 17.1% on SIMON dataset compared to the same model trained on FreeSurfer derived measurements. The results suggest that DL+DiReCT provides automatic labels more suitable for CTh estimation model training than FreeSurfer.

Keywords: Weak labels · Cortical thickness definition · Cortical thickness estimation · Model learning optimisation

This work was funded in part through an Australian Department of Industry, Energy and Resources CRC-P project between CSIRO, Maxwell Plus and I-Med Radiology Network.

H. V. Nguyen et al. (Eds.): DALI 2022, LNCS 13567, pp. 33–42, 2022.
https://doi.org/10.1007/978-3-031-17027-0_4

1   Introduction

Cortical thickness (CTh) is an important biomarker for the diagnosis and prognosis of neurodegenerative diseases, such as Alzheimer's disease (AD) [14]. Estimating and tracking CTh changes in a living brain may reveal insights into disease trajectory, quantitatively evaluate treatment effects, and enable correlations between brain regions and age, cognitive deterioration, genotype, or medication [1]. Despite the importance of CTh as a biomarker, a generally accepted gold standard for in-vivo CTh measurements currently does not exist [15]. An accepted gold standard does not exist as there is no standardised definition of CTh estimates and even if there was one, post-mortem histology measurements are unreliable [15]. In-vivo CTh measurements can only be estimated from human brain scans acquired using neuroimaging techniques such as magnetic resonance imaging (MRI) [9]. Manual CTh estimation from MRI scans is laborious, subjective and requires a high level of expertise which makes it infeasible in practice [7]. Therefore robust software tools such as FreeSurfer [6] are typically utilised for automatic CTh estimation from brain MRIs [21]. However, such tools are also time-consuming (FreeSurfer - up to 10 h per scan) since their CTh estimation relies on throughputs such as segmentation maps, partial volume maps, and triangular meshes that need to be constructed before estimation takes place [20]. Therefore, such tools are not adequate for clinical applications requiring timely results [20]. Recently, a couple of studies approached the problem of time-consuming automatic CTh, volume and curvature estimations by proposing Deep Learning (DL)-based solutions that reduce estimation time from hours to seconds at the expense of estimation accuracy [18,20]. Currently, DL-based methods [18,20] are trained and tested against FreeSurfer measurements that are considered to be the best approximation of the gold-standard ground truth, so called silver-standard. By doing so, these DL-based methods learn FreeSurfer-specific CTh definition bias as well as FreeSurfer software-specific biases coming from the method design and its implementation. While biases cannot be completely avoided due to a non-existing true bias-free gold-standard CTh measurements, the choice of CTh measurement for training may impact DL-model learning capabilities.

In this paper, we investigate the impact of the choice of automatic labels (CTh measurements) on the training of the state-of-the-art DL-based CTh estimation method - HerstonNet [20]. Firstly, we modify the original HerstonNet solution to decouple CTh from the other morphological estimations (volume and curvature). Then we train the decoupled HerstonNet solution on CTh measurements derived by FreeSurfer and DL+DiReCT [17] to ensure different CTh definition and method biases. Finally, we evaluate the trained models on three subsets of brain MRIs from four datasets ADNI, AIBL, OASIS and SIMON. The contributions of this paper are the following: i) insights into the impact of bias labels (CTh estimations) choice on the training of HerstonNet and ii) comparison in performance (intraclass correlation and test-retest) between HerstonNet trained with FreeSurfer (silver standard) and DL+DiReCT-derived CTh estimations on three datasets.

2   Methods

Data & Pre-processing. In this work, we used T1-weighted (T1-w) brain MRI scans from four datasets: Alzheimer's Disease Neuroimaging Initiative (ADNI)[1] [11,23] Australian Imaging, Biomarker and Lifestyle Flagship Study of Ageing (AIBL) [19], Open Access Series of Imaging Studies (OASIS) [13] and Single Individual volunteer for Multiple Observations across Networks (SIMON) [5]. The models under test were trained, validated and tested on a subset composed of 9310 MRIs from both ADNI and AIBL datasets. The subset was split into training, validation and test sets, roughly in the 60:15:25 ratio, respectively, with no overlap between subsets to avoid data leakage. Further insights into the subset, data split, demographics and pathologies are detailed in Table 1. The MRIs taken from ADNI and AIBL datasets were pre-processed by correcting the bias field in the brain region of interest (ROI) [22]. Further, 9310 bias-field corrected MRIs from ADNI and AIBL datasets, together with 2720 MRIs from OASIS-3 and 96 MRIs from SIMON datasets, were rigidly registered to MNI-space ($181 \times 217 \times 181$ voxels) and z-score intensity normalised with the mean value computed in the brain ROI. The MRIs from the OASIS-3 and SIMON datasets were used for testing only.

Automatic Cortical Thickness Measurements. In this work, we employed two CTh estimation tools, FreeSurfer cross-sectional pipeline [8] and DL+DiReCT [17]. FreeSurfer cross-sectional pipeline relies on the construction of white matter (WM) and grey matter (GM) surfaces to map morphometric mea-

Table 1. Insights into the train, validation and test subsets of ADNI and AIBL datasets, data split, demographics and pathology across subsets. S annotates the number of subjects while N stands for the number of data points. The column *Other* comprises subjects/data points with under-represented or unavailable pathology.

	Healthy Control (HC)		Mild Cognitive Impairment (MCI)		Alzheimer's Disease (AD)		Other	
	S	N	S	N	S	N	S	N
Train	441	1127	996	1972	537	922	1013	1611
Validation	113	284	243	487	157	268	242	352
Test	190	482	391	736	252	420	421	649
Overall	**744**	**1893**	**1630**	**3195**	**946**	**1610**	**1676**	**2612**
	Mean Age (± STD)	*% Female*	*Mean Age (± STD)*	*% Female*	*Mean Age (± STD)*	*% Female*	*Mean Age (± STD)*	*% Female*
Train	74.79 ± 6.42	55.01	73.98 ± 6.90	58.87	76.30 ± 5.72	69.20	72.74 ± 7.25	49.65
Validation	74.02 ± 7.35	72.18	74.03 ± 6.16	56.88	76.74 ± 6.23	71.27	73.27 ± 7.55	44.68
Test	73.58 ± 6.37	49.38	73.85 ± 6.23	59.24	76.16 ± 6.27	77.62	72.65 ± 7.22	43.33
Overall	**74.37 ± 6.57**	**56.15**	**73.96 ± 6.64**	**58.65**	**76.34 ± 5.95**	**71.74**	**72.80 ± 7.28**	**47.31**

---

[1] Data used in the preparation of this article were obtained from the Alzheimer's Disease Neuroimaging Initiative (ADNI) database (adni.loni.usc.edu). The ADNI was launched in 2003 as a public-private partnership, led by Principal Investigator Michael W. Weiner, MD. The primary goal of ADNI has been to test whether serial magnetic resonance imaging (MRI), positron emission tomography (PET), other biological markers, and clinical and neuropsychological assessment can be combined to measure the progression of mild cognitive impairment (MCI) and early AD. For up-to-date information, see www.adni-info.org [11,23].

surements on the reconstructed surface. Once WM and GM surfaces are recon-structed, FreeSurfer estimates CTh as an average minimum distance between vertices on GM and WM surfaces and vice versa. DL+DiReCT estimates CTh by segmenting neuroanatomy using a DL-based model called DeepSCAN [16] followed by diffeomorphic registration-based CTh (DiReCT) [3] measurements. DeepSCAN segments T1-w brain MRIs into GM and WM segmentation as well as parcellation, while DiReCT obtains CTh from MRIs and corresponding seg-mentations. DiReCT defines CTh as a distance measure between corresponding cerebrospinal fluid (CSF)/GM and GM/WM interfaces, where continuous one-to-one mapping is ensured by diffeomorphic registration [3,17].

HerstonNet, Modifications and Training. In this section, we focus on Her-stonNet [20], the state-of-the-art regression-based neural network for efficient brain morphometry analysis, and modifications we made to decouple the CTh estimation from the rest of the morphometry measurements. HerstonNet is a 3D ResNet-based neural network that learns rich features directly from MRI. Throughout the multi-scale regression scheme, HerstonNet predicts morphome-tric measures from feature maps of various resolutions, which robustly leverages the network optimisation to avoid poor quality minima and lower the predic-tion variance. Santa Cruz *et al.* trained HerstonNet on pairs of images, and FreeSurfer derived CTh, volume and curvature. Further, the authors employed a data-augmentation strategy by applying Gaussian noise injection, translations (up to 15 voxels), and rotations (up to 30°) on input brain MRIs. After 170 epochs of training, they apply Stochastic Weight Averaging (SWA) optimisation technique [10] to improve the generalisation of the model. In our experiments, we follow the architecture, training strategy, and data splits as described in [20] with a couple of major modifications. Instead of predicting the CTh, volume, and curvature, we modify the output size and restrict predictions to CTh only. Further, we skip the SWA step to emphasise the model generalisability differ-ence between models trained on different automatic CTh measurements. We trained the modified version of HerstonNet according to [20] with the difference in the number of epochs. Instead of training modified HerstonNet models for 170 epochs, we stopped training after 140 h (142 epochs) when both models' losses plateaued. Both models were optimised by minimising the mean squared error (MSE) on batches of six samples by employing the Adam optimiser with a learning rate 10^{-4}. We also followed the augmentation strategy detailed in [20].

3   Experiments and Results

Visualisation of CTh Measurement Difference. To better understand the difference between FreeSurfer and DL+DiReCT measurements, we mapped the region-wise mean absolute difference and standard deviation (STD) to the brain template meshes (Fig. 1). We considered 34 ROIs per hemisphere defined by the Desikan-Killiany atlas [4]. The mean absolute difference and the STD (in mm) were computed on the training set that comprises 5582 MRI scans from ADNI and AIBL datasets. According to Fig. 1, in the parietal lobe, we measured

The absolute difference in cortical thickness between FreeSurfer and DL+DiReCT (mm)

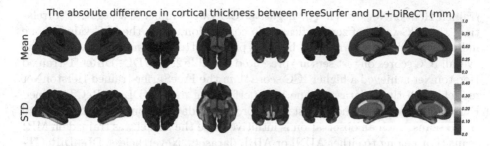

Fig. 1. The absolute CTh difference between FreeSurfer and DL+DiReCT computed on 5582 scans randomly selected from ADNI and AIBL datasets.

a mean absolute difference around 0.25 mm, while in the frontal and occipital lobes we measured minimal difference between the CTh estimations. In the temporal lobe, the methods predominantly differ in inferior temporal gyrus, banks of the superior temporal sulcus, fusiform gyrus, entorhinal cortex and temporal pole, where the difference in CTh estimations reaches 0.5 mm. Overall, the differences between the estimated CTh are mainly symmetric on both hemispheres. Given that the average CTh spans across regions in the [2.5 to 3] mm interval [9], the difference of up to 0.5 mm between the CTh estimation methods is significant. We confirmed the significance of CTh estimations difference in all 34 brain ROI on both hemispheres by performing a t-test followed by Bonferroni correction. In the context of model training, validation and testing, such a significant difference between FreeSurfer and DL+DiReCT CTh estimations imply that models should not be trained with FreeSurfer while being validated and tested with DL+DiReCT CTh estimations, and vice versa.

FreeSurfer-Trained vs. DL+DiReCT-Trained HerstonNet Model Estimations. To evaluate the impact of labels (CTh measurements) derived by FreeSurfer and DL+DiReCT on model learning and performance, we train two modified HerstonNet models, FreeSurfer-trained and DL+DiReCT-trained HerstonNet. FreeSurfer-trained HerstonNet was trained on pairs of brain MRIs and corresponding FreeSurfer CTh estimations, while the DL+DiReCT-trained HerstonNet was trained on pairs of brain MRIs and corresponding DL+DiReCT CTh estimations. Both models were trained on the same train set comprising 5582 MRIs from ADNI and AIBL datasets. Each training sample is represented with an MRI and corresponding CTh estimations of 68 regions (34 regions/hemisphere). Once trained, we tested both models on three different test sets, composed of ADNI+AIBL, OASIS and SIMON MRIs. For model performance evaluation, we used the intraclass correlation coefficient (ICC) as well as a 95% confidence interval. Based on the research reliability guidelines for ICC values reporting [12], we computed the two-way mixed effects, absolute agreement, and single rater (ICC(2,1)) between the predicted and either FreeSurfer CTh estimations as ground-truth in the case of FreeSurfer-trained HerstonNet and DL+DiReCT CTh estimations as ground-truth in the case of DL+DiReCT-trained HerstonNet model. The negative ICC values indicate a negative correlation, the ICC value of zero indicates no correlation, while the ICC value of one indicates the perfect correlation between predicted and ground truth values. The overall ICC scores on test sets are presented in Table 2. The DL+DiReCT-trained HerstonNet achieved a higher ICC score than the FreeSurfer-trained HerstonNet model on all three datasets. The best performing model (DL+DiReCT-trained HerstonNet) achieved the highest ICC score on the dataset composed of ADNI and AIBL scans. Such an observation is intuitive since the model was trained on MRI scans that belong to either ADNI or AIBL datasets. Nevertheless, DL+DiReCT-trained HerstonNet also achieved a higher ICC score on the other two datasets (OASIS-3 and SIMON), which were not involved in the training. Since both models were not exposed to any images from the OASIS-3 and SIMON datasets, the fact that DL+DiReCT-trained HerstonNet performed better than FreeSurfer-trained HerstonNet is a strong indication of higher generalisability. Overall, DL+DiReCT-trained HerstonNet achieved 13.3% higher ICC score than FreeSurfer-trained HerstonNet on the dataset composed of ADNI and AIBL MRIs, 19.4% higher ICC on the OASIS-3 dataset and 17.1% on SIMON dataset.

Table 2. The mean ICC value and standard deviation, computed over all 34 regions on both hemispheres, achieved by both modified HerstonNet models trained on pairs of MRI and either FreeSurfer or DL+DiReCT CTh estimates on three datasets: ADNI+AIBL, OASIS, and SIMON. The difference in achieved is expressed in %. The sign ↑ denotes that the higher metric values suggest better results.

Test set	Number of MRI scans	Intraclass Correlation Coefficient (ICC) ↑		Difference (%)
		HerstonNet (FreeSurfer)	HerstonNet (DL+DiReCT)	
ADNI + AIBL	2282	0.767 ± 0.093	**0.9 ± 0.047**	13.3%
OASIS-3	2720	0.227 ± 0.125	**0.421 ± 0.194**	19.4%
SIMON	96	0.122 ± 0.12	**0.293 ± 0.15**	17.1%

We also compared the region-wise achieved ICC scores and 95% confidence intervals of FreeSurfer-trained and DL+DiReCT-trained HerstonNet models. Based on the discussion provided in [2] and following [18, 20], we utilise the ICC intervals, commonly used in clinical applications. The ICC intervals are visualised at the bottom of Fig. 2. The comparison of ICC scores and 95% confidence intervals achieved by FreeSurfer-trained and DL+DiReCT-trained HerstonNet are visualised in Fig. 2. According to Fig. 2, DL+DiReCT-trained HerstonNet achieves higher ICC than FreeSurfer-trained HerstonNet in all 34 brain regions on both hemispheres. The mean ICC values achieved by DL+DiReCT-trained HerstonNet in all 34 brain regions on both hemispheres fall into the ICC ≥ 0.75 (excellent) ICC interval, while ICC values achieved by FreeSurfer-trained HerstonNet mainly fall into $0.6 \geq$ ICC < 0.75 (good) ICC interval. Further, DL+DiReCT-trained HerstonNet overall achieved tighter 95% confidence intervals than the FreeSurfer-trained HerstonNet model. There are six brain regions on both hemispheres where FreeSurfer-trained HerstonNet achieved tighter 95% confidence intervals than DL+DiReCT-trained HerstonNet. The six brain regions

Cortical Thickness

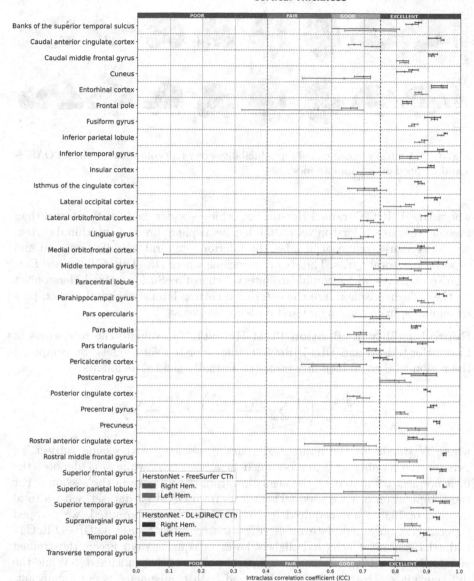

Fig. 2. ICC scores with 95% confidence intervals, computed on 2282 MRIs coming from ADNI and AIBL datasets, for FreeSurfer-trained and DL+DiReCT-trained HerstonNet CTh estimations in 34 cortical regions per hemisphere.

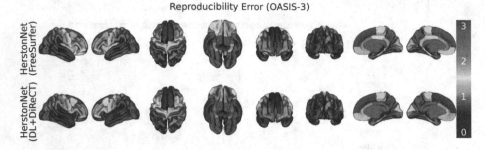

Fig. 3. Test-retest - colour coded reproducibility error (%) computed on subset OASIS-3 and mapped on a template mesh.

where DL+DiReCT-trained HerstonNet achieves wider confidence interval than FreeSurfer-trained HerstonNet on the left hemisphere are the entorhinal cortex, pars opercularis, paracentral lobe, the inferior temporal, middle temporal and superior temporal gyrus. The six brain regions where DL+DiReCT-trained HerstonNet achieves wider confidence interval than FreeSurfer-trained HerstonNet on the right hemisphere are the entorhinal cortex, lateral occipital cortex, pars triangularis, fusiform, lingual and postcentral gyrus.

Reproducibility Evaluation (Test-Retest). To evaluate the robustness of FreeSurfer-trained and DL+DiReCT-trained HerstonNet models, we computed the region-wise reproducibility error (ϵ), formally defined as follows:

$$\epsilon = \frac{100}{N} \sum_{i=1}^{N} \left(\frac{1}{n_i} \sum_{t=1}^{n_i} \frac{|\mu_{i,t} - \mu_i|}{\mu_i} \right), \mu_i = \frac{1}{n_i} \sum_{t=1}^{n_i} m_{i,t} \tag{1}$$

where N stands for the number of scanning sessions of the same subject, n_i denotes the number of scans obtained in a session i, while $m_{i,t}$ denotes the measurement computed by the algorithm from the tth scan in the session i. For the computation of ϵ we used 592 subjects from OASIS-3 dataset, with a total number of 1536 scans acquired in 757 sessions. Once computed, we mapped ϵ per region on a template mesh (Fig. 3). According to Fig. 3, DL+DiReCT-trained HerstonNet achieved slightly lower or equal ϵ than FreeSurfer-trained HerstonNet in all regions except temporal pol on both hemispheres. While the difference in ϵ across 34 brain regions and both hemispheres is not significant, such an outcome suggests higher reliability of DL+DiReCT-trained HerstonNet over FreeSurfer-trained HerstonNet.

4　Conclusion

In this paper, we investigated the benefits of using two different automatic CTh estimations for the training of HerstonNet - the state-of-the-art DL-based model for direct CTh estimation from brain MRIs. The obtained results indicate that training HerstonNet on DL+DiReCT CTh estimations makes the model more generalisable and robust when compared with HerstonNet trained on FreeSurfer CTh. However, more experiments are needed to evaluate whether such a conclusion is generalisable to other automatic CTh estimations, DL-based models and datasets. For future work, we plan to thoroughly investigate the impact of several automatic CTh estimations on the training of DL models as well as the main drivers behind the learning acceleration.

References

1. Aganj, I., Sapiro, G., Parikshak, N., Madsen, S.K., Thompson, P.M.: Measurement of cortical thickness from MRI by minimum line integrals on soft-classified tissue. Human Brain Mapp. **30**(10), 3188–3199 (2009)
2. Cicchetti, D.V.: Guidelines, criteria, and rules of thumb for evaluating normed and standardized assessment instruments in psychology. Psychol. Assessm. **6**(4), 284 (1994)
3. Das, S.R., Avants, B.B., Grossman, M., Gee, J.C.: Registration based cortical thickness measurement. Neuroimage **45**(3), 867–879 (2009)
4. Desikan, R.S.,et al.: An automated labeling system for subdividing the human cerebral cortex on MRI scans into Gyral based regions of interest. Neuroimage **31**(3), 968–980 (2006)
5. Duchesne, S., et al.: Structural and functional multi-platform MRI series of a single human volunteer over more than fifteen years. Sci. Data **6**(1), 1–9 (2019)
6. Fischl, B.: Freesurfer. Neuroimage **62**(2), 774–781 (2012)
7. Fischl, B., Dale, A.M.: Measuring the thickness of the human cerebral cortex from magnetic resonance images. Proc. Natl. Acad. Sci. **97**(20), 11050–11055 (2000)
8. Fischl, B., Sereno, M.I., Dale, A.M.: Cortical surface-based analysis: Ii: inflation, flattening, and a surface-based coordinate system. Neuroimage **9**(2), 195–207 (1999)
9. Hutton, C., De Vita, E., Ashburner, J., Deichmann, R., Turner, R.: Voxel-based cortical thickness measurements in MRI. Neuroimage **40**(4), 1701–1710 (2008)
10. Izmailov, P., Podoprikhin, D., Garipov, T., Vetrov, D., Wilson, A.G.: Averaging weights leads to wider optima and better generalization. arXiv preprint arXiv:1803.05407 (2018)
11. Jack, C.R., Jr., et al.: The Alzheimer's disease neuroimaging initiative (ADNI): MRI methods. J. Magnet. Resonan. Imag. Off. J. Int. Soc. Magnet. Resonan. Med. **27**(4), 685–691 (2008)
12. Koo, T.K., Li, M.Y.: A guideline of selecting and reporting intraclass correlation coefficients for reliability research. J. Chiropract. Med. **15**(2), 155–163 (2016)
13. LaMontagne, P.J., et al.: Oasis-3: longitudinal neuroimaging, clinical, and cognitive dataset for normal aging and Alzheimer disease. MedRxiv (2019)
14. Li, Q., Pardoe, H., Lichter, R., Werden, E., Raffelt, A., Cumming, T., Brodtmann, A.: Cortical thickness estimation in longitudinal stroke studies: a comparison of 3 measurement methods. NeuroImage Clin. **8**, 526–535 (2015)
15. Lüsebrink, F., Wollrab, A., Speck, O.: Cortical thickness determination of the human brain using high resolution 3 t and 7 t MRI data. Neuroimage **70**, 122–131 (2013)
16. McKinley, R., et al.: Simultaneous lesion and brain segmentation in multiple sclerosis using deep neural networks. Sci. Rep. **11**(1), 1–11 (2021)

17. Rebsamen, M., Rummel, C., Reyes, M., Wiest, R., McKinley, R.: Direct cortical thickness estimation using deep learning-based anatomy segmentation and cortex parcellation. Human Brain Mapp. **41**(17), 4804–4814 (2020)
18. Rebsamen, M., Suter, Y., Wiest, R., Reyes, M., Rummel, C.: Brain morphometry estimation: from hours to seconds using deep learning. Front. Neurol. **11**, 244 (2020)
19. Rowe, C.C., et al.: Amyloid imaging results from the Australian imaging, biomarkers and lifestyle (AIBL) study of aging. Neurobiol. Aging **31**(8), 1275–1283 (2010)
20. Santa Cruz, R., et al.: Going deeper with brain morphometry using neural networks. In: 2021 IEEE 18th International Symposium on Biomedical Imaging (ISBI), pp. 711–715. IEEE (2021)
21. Tustison, N.J., et al.: Large-scale evaluation of ants and freesurfer cortical thickness measurements. Neuroimage **99**, 166–179 (2014)
22. Van Leemput, K., Maes, F., Vandermeulen, D., Suetens, P.: Automated model-based bias field correction of MR images of the brain. IEEE Trans. Med. Imaging **18**(10), 885–896 (1999)
23. Weiner, M.W., et al.: The Alzheimer's disease neuroimaging initiative 3: continued innovation for clinical trial improvement. Alzheimer's Dementia **13**(5), 561–571 (2017)

TAAL: Test-Time Augmentation for Active Learning in Medical Image Segmentation

Mélanie Gaillochet(✉), Christian Desrosiers, and Hervé Lombaert

ETS Montréal, Montréal, Canada
melanie.gaillochet.1@ens.etsmtl.ca

Abstract. Deep learning methods typically depend on the availability of labeled data, which is expensive and time-consuming to obtain. Active learning addresses such effort by prioritizing which samples are best to annotate in order to maximize the performance of the task model. While frameworks for active learning have been widely explored in the context of classification of natural images, they have been only sparsely used in medical image segmentation. The challenge resides in obtaining an uncertainty measure that reveals the best candidate data for annotation. This paper proposes Test-time Augmentation for Active Learning (TAAL), a novel semi-supervised active learning approach for segmentation that exploits the uncertainty information offered by data transformations. Our method applies cross-augmentation consistency during training and inference to both improve model learning in a semi-supervised fashion and identify the most relevant unlabeled samples to annotate next. In addition, our consistency loss uses a modified version of the JSD to further improve model performance. By relying on data transformations rather than on external modules or simple heuristics typically used in uncertainty-based strategies, TAAL emerges as a simple, yet powerful task-agnostic semi-supervised active learning approach applicable to the medical domain. Our results on a publicly-available dataset of cardiac images show that TAAL outperforms existing baseline methods in both fully-supervised and semi-supervised settings. Our implementation is publicly available on https://github.com/melinphd/TAAL.

1 Introduction

The performance of deep learning-based models improves as the number of labeled training samples increases. Yet, the burden of annotation limits the amount of data that can be labeled. One solution to that problem is offered by active learning (AL) [1]. Based on the hypothesis that all data samples have a different impact on training, active learning aims to find the best set of candidate samples to annotate in order to maximize the performance of the task model. In such context, medical image segmentation emerges as a remarkably relevant task for active learning. Indeed, medical images typically require prior expert knowledge for their analysis and annotation, an expensive and time-consuming task. Initial attempts have explored active learning in medical imaging [2], but their methodology either relied on simple uncertainty heuristics [3,4] or required heavy computations during sampling [5,6] or training [7].

Deep Active Learning. Active learning has been extensively explored for the classification [8–13] or segmentation [14–16] of natural images. Recent deep active learning approaches based on entropy [12] or ensembles [9] adapted traditional uncertainty-based AL strategies to deep learning models. Similarly, DBAL [10] combined measures such as entropy or mutual information with Monte-Carlo dropout to suggest which samples to annotate next. Core-set selection [11] aimed to find the best batch sampling strategy for CNNs in classification, but did not scale well to high-dimensional data.

The use of auxiliary modules [13,17,18] has been similarly explored to improve AL sampling strategies. The loss prediction module of [13] measured model uncertainty with intermediate representations. Likewise, a VAE was used in VAAL [17] to learn the latent representation of the unlabeled dataset and distinguish between labeled and unlabeled samples. While these state-of-the-art methods have improved previous approaches, their dependence on auxiliary modules reduces their flexibility and increase the burden of hyperparameter tuning.

Semi-supervised AL. Semi-supervised learning (SSL) exploits the representations of unlabeled data to improve the performance of the task model. Since semi-supervised learning and active learning are closely connected, recent works in AL have attempted to combine both domains [12,17–19]. For instance, CEAL [12] used pseudo-labeling of unlabeled samples to enhance the labeled set during training. VAAL [17] and TA-VAAL [18] employed a VAE to learn a latent representation of labeled and unlabeled data. The Mean Teacher framework of [19] combined a supervised loss on labeled data with an unsupervised loss on unlabeled data based on Temporal Output Discrepancy (TOD), evaluating the distance between the model's output at different gradient steps. The model used a variant of TOD at sampling time to identify the most uncertain samples to annotate. However, these semi-supervised AL methods solely focused on classification tasks or the segmentation of natural images in very large quantities, which is a different context than medical imaging. Another recent work comparable to ours combined AL and SSL via consistency regularization [20]. The consistency loss adopted during training employed MixMatch [21] and sample selection measured inconsistency across input perturbations. However, as opposed to our work, [20] kept the consistency loss used during training and the AL inconsistency metric used for sample selection independent of each other, and the latter was quantified through variance. Furthermore, the method was only validated on classification tasks.

Test-Time Augmentation. Data augmentation is a well-known regularization technique to improve generalization in low-data regimes. These augmentation techniques are particularly essential in medical imaging where datasets tend to be smaller than those of natural images. Yet most recent attempts in active learning do not exploit data augmentation during training [6,8], or only use random horizontal flipping [17,18]. Recent learning methods [22,23] have also investigated the use of augmentation at test-time in order evaluate prediction uncertainty. Randomly augmented test images yield different model outputs. Combining these outputs can improve the overall predictions as well as generate uncertainty maps for these predictions. Uncertainty estimated through test-time augmentation was shown to be more reliable than model uncertainty measures such as test-time dropout or entropy of the output [23].

Motivated by the limitations of current active learning methods for medical image segmentation and the unused potential of active augmentation, this paper proposes a novel semi-supervised active learning strategy called Test-time Augmentation for Active Learning (TAAL).

Our Contribution. Our method leverages the uncertainty information provided by data augmentation during both training and test-time sample selection phases. More specifically, TAAL employs a cross-augmentation consistency loss both to train the model in a semi-supervised fashion *as well as* to identify the most uncertain samples to annotate at the next cycle. TAAL comprises three key features:

1. a semi-supervised framework based on cross-augmentation consistency that exploits unlabeled samples during training and sampling;
2. a flexible task-agnostic sample selection strategy based on test-time augmentation;
3. a novel uncertainty measure based on a modified Jensen-Shannon divergence (JSD), which accounts for both cross-augmentation consistency and prediction entropy, and leads to improved performance.

2   Method

Cross-augmentation Consistency Training. We consider a semi-supervised setting where we train a multi-class segmentation model $f_\theta(\cdot)$ parameterized by θ with N labeled samples and M unlabeled samples. We denote the labeled set as $\mathcal{D}_L = \{(\mathbf{x}^{(j)}, \mathbf{y}^{(j)})\}_{j=1}^{N}$ and the unlabeled set as $\mathcal{D}_U = \{\mathbf{x}_u^{(j)}\}_{j=1}^{M}$, with data $\mathbf{x}, \mathbf{x}_u \in \mathbb{R}^{H \times W}$ and segmentation mask $\mathbf{y} \in \mathbb{R}^{C \times H \times W}$ (C is the number of classes).

The overall loss that we optimize, $\mathcal{L} = \mathcal{L}_s + \lambda \mathcal{L}_c$, is a combination of a supervised segmentation loss $\mathcal{L}_s$ and an unsupervised consistency loss $\mathcal{L}_c$ weighted by a factor λ. More explicitly, the objective is defined as

$$\mathcal{L} = \frac{1}{N} \sum_{j=1}^{N} \mathcal{L}_s\big(f_\theta(\mathbf{x}^{(j)}), \mathbf{y}^{(j)}\big) + \frac{\lambda}{M} \sum_{j=1}^{M} \mathcal{L}_c\big(f_\theta(\mathbf{x}_u^{(j)}), \Gamma\big), \qquad (1)$$

where Γ are the transformations applied to $\mathbf{x}_u^{(j)}$. At each iteration, we apply a series of random transformations $\{\Gamma_1, ..., \Gamma_K\}$ to $\mathbf{x}_u$. $\mathcal{L}_c$ measures the variability of segmentation predictions for different augmentations of $\mathbf{x}_u$ measured by a function $\mathcal{D}iv$:

$$\mathcal{L}_c\big(f_\theta(\mathbf{x}_u^{(j)}), \Gamma\big) = \mathcal{D}iv\{\Gamma_1^{-1}[f_\theta(\Gamma_1(\mathbf{x}_u^{(j)}))], \dots, \Gamma_K^{-1}[f_\theta(\Gamma_K(\mathbf{x}_u^{(j)}))]\}. \quad (2)$$

While different measures can be used for $\mathcal{D}iv$ [24], our consistency loss builds on the Jensen Shannon divergence (JSD),

$$\mathrm{JSD}(P_1, \dots, P_K) = H\big(\frac{1}{K}\sum_{i=i}^{K} P_i\big) - \frac{1}{K}\sum_{i=i}^{K} H(P_i), \quad (3)$$

where $H(P_i)$ is the Shannon entropy [25] for the probability distributions P_i. Minimizing the JSD reduces the entropy of the average prediction (making the predictions more similar to each other) while increasing the average of individual prediction entropies (ensuring confident predictions). In AL we typically want to select samples which have a high output entropy [12]. Selecting samples with highest JSD would thus have the opposite effect. To avoid this issue, and to control the relative importance of average prediction entropy versus entropy of individual predictions, we propose a weighted version of JSD with parameter α.

$$\mathrm{JSD}_\alpha(P_1, \dots, P_K) = \alpha H\big(\frac{1}{K}\sum_{i=i}^{K} P_i\big) - \frac{(1-\alpha)}{K}\sum_{i=i}^{K} H(P_i). \quad (4)$$

Note that using $\alpha = 0.5$ is equivalent to using the standard JSD.

Test-Time Augmentation Sampling. In active learning, the goal is to select the best unlabeled samples to annotate after each training cycle to augment the next labeled training set. Hence, after each cycle, we apply our active learning strategy based on test-time augmentation to select the next samples to annotate.

For each sample $\mathbf{x}_u \in \mathcal{D}_U$, we apply a series of transformations $\{\Gamma_1', \dots, \Gamma_{K_s}'\}$, and we compute an uncertainty score $U_{\Gamma'}$ based on the same divergence function as the consistency loss:

$$U_{\Gamma'} = \mathrm{JSD}_\alpha\big(\Gamma_1'^{-1}[f_\theta(\Gamma_1'(\mathbf{x}_u))], \dots, \Gamma_{K_s}'^{-1}[f_\theta(\Gamma_{K_s}'(\mathbf{x}_u))]\big). \quad (5)$$

The samples with highest uncertainty are annotated and added to the labeled training set. After sample selection, the model goes through a new training cycle.

3 Experiments and Results

3.1 Implementation Details

Dataset. The publicly available ACDC dataset [26] comprises cardiac 3D cine-MRI scans from 100 patients. These are evenly distributed into 5 groups (4 pathological and 1 healthy subjects groups). Segmentation masks identify 4 regions of interest: right-ventricle cavity, left-ventricle cavity, myocardium and background. For comparative purposes, our experiments focus on the MRI scans at the end of diastole. Preprocessing of the volumes includes resampling to a fixed 1.0 mm × 1.0 mm resolution in the x- and y-directions as well as a 99th percentile normalization. The 3-dimensional dataset of volumes are converted to a 2-dimensional dataset of images by extracting all the z-axis slices for each volume. Each image is downsampled to 128 × 128 pixels. Testing is performed on 181 images taken from 20 different patients, ensuring subjects are not split up across training and testing sets. The validation uses 100 randomly selected images. The same validation set is used for all experiments. In total, the available training set, both labeled and unlabeled, thus comprises 660 images.

Implementation and Training. We employ a standard 4-layer UNet [27] for our backbone segmentation model with dropout (p = 0.5), batch normalization and a leaky ReLU activation function. For a fairer comparison in our experiments, we keep the number of training steps fixed during all cycles. We train our models for 75 epochs, each iterating over 250 batches, with $BS = 4$. We use the Adam optimizer [28], with $LR = 10^{-6}$ and weight decay $w = 10^{-4}$. To improve convergence, we apply a gradual warmup with a cosine annealing scheduler [29,30], increasing the learning rate by a factor 200 during the first 10 epochs. During training, we apply data augmentation, using transformations similar to those utilized for the consistency loss.

In this work, we model the transformations Γ as a combination of f, r and ϵ, where f is the random variable for flipping the image along the horizontal axis, r is the number of 90° rotations in 2D, and ϵ models Gaussian noise. We set $f \sim \mathcal{U}(0,1)$, $r \sim \mathcal{U}(0,3)$ and $\epsilon \sim \mathcal{N}(0,0.01)$, and use $K = 3$ transformations to compute the consistency loss during training.

We use the standard Dice loss as our supervised loss. In the semi-supervised case, following [31], we ramp-up the unsupervised component weight using a Gaussian ramp-up curve such that $\lambda = \exp(-5(1-t/t_R)^2)$, where t is the current epoch. We use a ramp-up length t_R of 10 epochs, corresponding to the learning rate gradual warmup length.

We repeat each experiment 5 times, each with a different seed determining different initialization of our model weights. For all experiments, the same initial labeled set is used for the first cycle. Experiments were run on NVIDIA P100 and V100 GPU with CUDA 10.2 and Python 3.8.10. We implemented the methods using the PyTorch framework.

Evaluation Metrics. To evaluate the performance of the trained models, we employ the standard Dice similarity score, averaged over all non-background channels. We compute both the mean 3D Dice on test volumes and mean 2D Dice on the individual images from these volumes. We give the results as the mean Dice obtained over the repeated experiments.

3.2 Active Learning Setup

We begin each experiment with 10 labeled samples chosen uniformly at random in the training set and use a sampling budget of 1, meaning that we select one new sample to be labeled after each cycle. Following previous active learning validation settings [11], we retrain the model from scratch after each annotation cycle. We use the same types of augmentations during training and sample selection. For test-time augmentation (TTA) sampling, $\{\Gamma'_1, \ldots, \Gamma'_{K_s}\}$ comprises all 8 combinations of flip and rotation augmentations, in order to apply similar transformations to all images, and adopts the same augmentation Gaussian noise parameters as for training. For comparative purposes, with dropout-based sampling, we also run 8 inferences with dropout to obtain different predictions. Both TTA and dropout-based sampling then evaluate uncertainty with $U_{\Gamma'}$ computed on the different generated predictions. We set $\alpha = 0.75$ in TAAL's weighted JSD.

3.3 Comparison of Active Learning Strategies

Our aim is to evaluate the effectiveness of our proposed semi-supervised active learning approach on a medical image segmentation task. In our active learning experiments, we compare TAAL and its unweighted version (with standard JSD) with random sampling, entropy sampling, sampling based on dropout and core-set selection. Entropy-based sampling selects the most uncertain samples based on the entropy of the output probabilities. Dropout-based sampling [10] identifies the samples with the highest JSD given multiple inferences with dropout. Finally, core-set selection [11] aims to obtain the most diverse labeled set by solving the maximum cover-set problem.

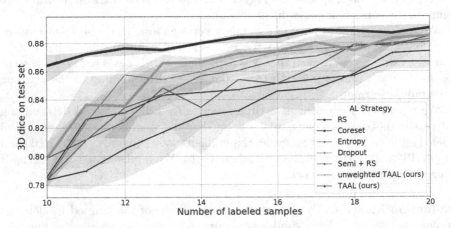

Fig. 1. Active learning results on the ACDC dataset, given as the mean 3D Dice scores on the test set and corresponding 95% confidence interval. In a fully-supervised setting: random sampling (RS), core-set selection (Coreset), uncertainty-based sampling based on entropy of output probabilities (Entropy), and uncertainty-based sampling based on JSD given multiple inferences with dropout (Dropout). In a semi-supervised setting: random sampling (Semi+RS), TAAL with standard JSD (unweighted TAAL), and TAAL with weighted JSD (TAAL). Our approach TAAL demonstrates significant improvements for low-data regimes in both fully and semi-supervised segmentation.

Figure 1 shows the segmentation performance of our proposed method with its 2 variants along with other existing active learning methods. TAAL consistently outperforms the other baselines by a large margin. We observe that our semi-supervised approach based on cross-augmentation consistency (Semi+RS) noticeably improves the fully-supervised vanilla model (RS). We notice that our unweighted version of TAAL (with standard JSD, $\alpha = 0.5$) already improves the performance of the semi-supervised model (Semi+RS) by selecting the most uncertain samples based on their cross-augmentation consistency loss. With higher $\alpha = 0.75$, our proposed TAAL with weighted JSD yields the highest performance gain compared to the fully-supervised vanilla model with random sampling (RS).

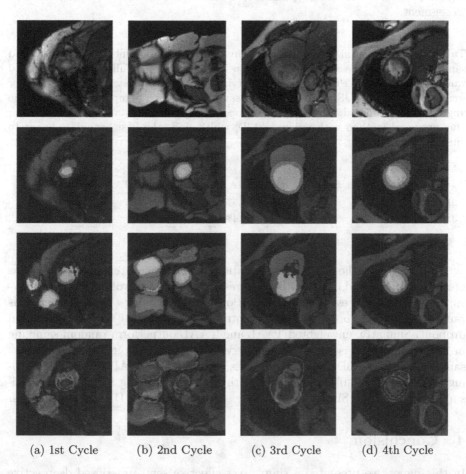

(a) 1st Cycle   (b) 2nd Cycle   (c) 3rd Cycle   (d) 4th Cycle

Fig. 2. Examples of images sampled by TAAL at different AL cycles. Are depicted the image sampled (row 1), the ground-truth segmentation (row 2), the segmentation prediction (row 3), and the JSD map given the different predictions from the augmented image (row 4). We observe that TAAL initially selected images with a large amount of hallucinated inaccurate predictions.

Figure 2 shows examples of images sampled by TAAL during the first 4 annotation cycles. TAAL initially selects image slices which show the apex of the heart. These samples are more difficult to learn in early stages since the areas to segment are much smaller than in the central slices of the heart and the image qualities are typically of lesser quality due to partial volume effects. Thus, we see that the choice of TAAL is first directed at samples yielding highly inaccurate predictions. The previous model has in fact even hallucinated multiple false segmentations for these samples as seen on the third row of Fig. 2a and 2b. In the next cycles, TAAL selects more central cardiac slices, which have improved predictions when compared to the ground-truth annotations. Hence, TAAL seems to first focus on correcting inaccurate predictions, before sharpening its predictions on a fine-grained level for slices with more prominent areas to segment.

Table 1. Active learning performances after doubling the number of initial labeled samples. We show the mean 2D and mean 3D Dice scores. 'Fully': Fully-supervised vanilla UNet. 'Semi': Proposed semi-supervised training with standard ($\alpha = 0.5$) or weighted ($\alpha = 0.75$) JSD. 'RS': Random sampling. 'TTA': Sampling with Test-time augmentation. 'unweighted TAAL': Our proposed method with standard JSD. 'TAAL': Our proposed method with weighted JSD, which finds the best candidate image to annotate.

Metric	Fully					Semi ($\alpha = 0.5$)		Semi ($\alpha = 0.75$)
	RS	Coreset	Entropy	Dropout	TTA	RS	Unweighted TAAL	TAAL
2D Dice	80.69	79.95	80.99	81.32	81.67	81.51	81.90	**82.51**
3D Dice	87.40	86.65	88.07	88.24	88.48	88.48	88.50	**89.06**

Table 1 gathers the model's segmentation performance after 10 cycles in terms of mean 2D Dice and mean 3D Dice scores over whole test volumes. In the fully-supervised setting, test-time augmentation-based sampling (TTA) outperforms random sampling, core-set selection, entropy sampling and sampling based on dropout. Similarly, unweighted TAAL and TAAL outperform random sampling in both semi-supervised and fully-supervised settings. After labeling 10 extra samples, the mean 3D Dice score attains 89.06% with TAAL while only reaching respectively 87.40% and 88.48% with random sampling in fully- and semi-supervised settings. Similar results were observed with 2D Dice on test images.

4   Conclusion

In this paper, we presented a simple, yet effective semi-supervised deep active learning approach for medical image segmentation. Our method, Test-time Augmentation for Active Learning (TAAL), employs a cross-augmentation consistency framework that produces both an improved training due to its unsupervised consistency loss, and a better sampling method through the uncertainty measure it provides. TAAL also uses a modified JSD that significantly improves the model's performance. Our results on the ACDC cardiac segmentation dataset show that, with TAAL, the trained model can reach up to 89.06% 3D Dice with 20 labeled samples when it only reaches 87.40% with random sampling. Because our approach exploits standard augmentation techniques already used in medical image segmentation tasks, TAAL emerges as a simple, yet efficient semi-supervised active learning strategy. While our method highly depends on the presence of disagreeing predictions for augmented inputs to identify the most informative samples, our observed improvements on a cardiac MRI dataset highlight promising avenues for future work, notably the investigation of more complex datasets and types of augmentations.

Acknowledgments. This work is supported by the Canada Research Chair on Shape Analysis in Medical Imaging, and the Research Council of Canada (NSERC). Computational resources were partially provided by Compute Canada. The authors also thank the ACDC Challenge organizers for providing the data.

References

1. Settles, B.: Active Learning Literature Survey. Technical Report, University of Wisconsin-Madison Department of Computer Sciences (2009)
2. Budd, S., Robinson, E.C., Kainz, B.: A survey on active learning and human-in-the-loop deep learning for medical image analysis. Med. Image Anal. **71**, 102062 (2021)
3. Top, A., Hamarneh, G., Abugharbieh, R.: Active learning for interactive 3D image segmentation. In: Fichtinger, G., Martel, A., Peters, T. (eds.) MICCAI 2011. LNCS, vol. 6893, pp. 603–610. Springer, Heidelberg (2011). https://doi.org/10.1007/978-3-642-23626-6_74
4. Konyushkova, K., Sznitman, R., Fua, P.: Geometry in active learning for binary and multi-class image segmentation. Comput. Vis. Image Understand. **182**, 1–16 (2019)
5. Sourati, J., Gholipour, A., Dy, J.G., Tomas-Fernandez, X., Kurugol, S., Warfield, S.K.: Intelligent labeling based on fisher information for medical image segmentation using deep learning. IEEE Trans. Med. Imaging **38**(11), 2642–2653 (2019)
6. Nath, V., Yang, D., Landman, B.A., Xu, D., Roth, H.R.: Diminishing Uncertainty within the training pool: active learning for medical image segmentation. IEEE Trans. Med. Imaging (2020)
7. Yang, L., Zhang, Y., Chen, J., Zhang, S., Chen, D.Z.: Suggestive annotation: a deep active learning framework for biomedical image segmentation. In: Descoteaux, M., Maier-Hein, L., Franz, A., Jannin, P., Collins, D.L., Duchesne, S. (eds.) MICCAI 2017. LNCS, vol. 10435, pp. 399–407. Springer, Cham (2017). https://doi.org/10.1007/978-3-319-66179-7_46
8. Ash, J.T., Zhang, C., Krishnamurthy, A., Langford, J., Agarwal, A.: Deep batch active learning by diverse, uncertain gradient lower bounds. In: Eighth International Conference on Learning Representations (ICLR) (2020)
9. Beluch, W.H., Genewein, T., Nurnberger, A., Kohler, J.M.: The power of ensembles for active learning in image classification. In: IEEE Conference on Computer Vision and Pattern Recognition (CVPR), pp. 9368–9377 (2018)

10. Gal, Y., Islam, R., Ghahramani, Z.: Deep Bayesian active learning with image data. In: Proceedings of the 34th International Conference on Machine Learning (ICML), pp. 1183–1192 (2017)
11. Sener, O., Savarese, S.: Active learning for convolutional neural networks: a core-set approach. In: International Conference on Learning Representations (ICLR) (2018)
12. Wang, K., Zhang, D., Li, Y., Zhang, R., Lin, L.: Cost-effective active learning for deep image classification. IEEE Trans. Circuits Syst. Video Technol. **27**(12), 2591–2600 (2017)
13. Yoo, D., Kweon, I.S.: Learning loss for active learning. In: IEEE Conference on Computer Vision and Pattern Recognition (CVPR), pp. 93–102 (2019)
14. Vezhnevets, A., Buhmann, J.M., Ferrari, V.: Active learning for semantic segmentation with expected change. In: IEEE Conference on Computer Vision and Pattern Recognition, pp. 3162–3169. IEEE (2012)
15. Siddiqui, Y., Valentin, J., Nießner, M.: Viewal: active learning with viewpoint entropy for semantic segmentation. In: Proceedings of the IEEE/CVF Conference on Computer Vision and Pattern Recognition, pp. 9433–9443 (2020)
16. Casanova, A., Pinheiro, P.O., Rostamzadeh, N., Pal, C.J.: Reinforced active learning for image segmentation. In: International Conference on Learning Representations (2019)
17. Sinha, S., Ebrahimi, S., Darrell, T.: Variational adversarial active learning. In: IEEE/CVF International Conference on Computer Vision (ICCV), pp. 5971–5980 (2019)
18. Kim, K., Park, D., Kim, K.I., Chun, S.Y.: Task-aware variational adversarial active learning. In: IEEE Conference on Computer Vision and Pattern Recognition (CVPR), pp. 8166–8175 (2021)
19. Huang, S., Wang, T., Xiong, H., Huan, J., Dou, D.: Semi-supervised active learning with temporal output discrepancy. In: Proceedings of the IEEE/CVF International Conference on Computer Vision (ICCV), pp. 3447–3456 (2021)
20. Gao, M., Zhang, Z., Yu, G., Arık, S., Davis, L.S., Pfister, T.: Consistency-based semi-supervised active learning: towards minimizing labeling cost. In: Vedaldi, A., Bischof, H., Brox, T., Frahm, J.-M. (eds.) ECCV 2020. LNCS, vol. 12355, pp. 510–526. Springer, Cham (2020). https://doi.org/10.1007/978-3-030-58607-2_30
21. Berthelot, D., Carlini, N., Goodfellow, I., Papernot, N., Oliver, A., Raffel, C.A.: MixMatch: a holistic approach to semi-supervised learning. In: Advances in Neural Information Processing Systems (NeurIPS), vol. 32. Curran Associates, Inc. (2019)
22. Ayhan, M.S., Berens, P.: Test-time data augmentation for estimation of heteroscedastic aleatoric uncertainty in deep neural networks (2018)
23. Wang, G., Li, W., Aertsen, M., Deprest, J., Ourselin, S., Vercauteren, T.: Aleatoric uncertainty estimation with test-time augmentation for medical image segmentation with convolutional neural networks. Neurocomputing **338**, 34–45 (2019)
24. Camarasa, R., et al.: Quantitative comparison of Monte-Carlo dropout uncertainty measures for multi-class segmentation. In: Sudre, C.H., et al. (eds.) UNSURE/GRAIL -2020. LNCS, vol. 12443, pp. 32–41. Springer, Cham (2020). https://doi.org/10.1007/978-3-030-60365-6_4
25. Shannon, C.E.: A mathematical theory of communication. Bell Syst. Tech. J. **27**(3), 379–423 (1948)
26. Bernard, O., et al.: Deep learning techniques for automatic MRI cardiac multi-structures segmentation and diagnosis: is the problem solved? IEEE Trans. Med. Imaging **37**(11), 2514–2525 (2018)

27. Ronneberger, O., Fischer, P., Brox, T.: U-Net: convolutional networks for biomedical image segmentation. In: Navab, N., Hornegger, J., Wells, W.M., Frangi, A.F. (eds.) MICCAI 2015. LNCS, vol. 9351, pp. 234–241. Springer, Cham (2015). https://doi.org/10.1007/978-3-319-24574-4_28
28. Kingma, D., Ba, J.: Adam: a method for stochastic optimization. In: International Conference on Learning Representations (ICLR) (2014)
29. Loshchilov, I., Hutter, F.: SGDR: stochastic gradient descent with warm restarts. In: International Conference on Learning Representations (ICLR) (2017)
30. Goyal, P., et al.: Accurate, Large Minibatch SGD: Training ImageNet in 1 Hour. arXiv:1706.02677 (2018)
31. Cui, W., et al.: Semi-supervised brain lesion segmentation with an adapted mean teacher model. In: Chung, A.C.S., Gee, J.C., Yushkevich, P.A., Bao, S. (eds.) Information Processing in Medical Imaging, LNCS, pp. 554–565. Springer, Cham (2019)

Disentangling a Single MR Modality

Lianrui Zuo[1,2(✉)], Yihao Liu[1], Yuan Xue[1], Shuo Han[3], Murat Bilgel[2],
Susan M. Resnick[2], Jerry L. Prince[1], and Aaron Carass[1]

[1] Department of Electrical and Computer Engineering, Johns Hopkins University,
Baltimore, MD 21218, USA
lr_zuo@jhu.edu
[2] Laboratory of Behavioral Neuroscience, National Institute on Aging,
National Institutes of Health, Baltimore, MD 20892, USA
[3] Department of Biomedical Engineering, Johns Hopkins School of Medicine,
Baltimore, MD 21287, USA

Abstract. Disentangling anatomical and contrast information from medical images has gained attention recently, demonstrating benefits for various image analysis tasks. Current methods learn disentangled representations using either paired multi-modal images with the same underlying anatomy or auxiliary labels (e.g., manual delineations) to provide inductive bias for disentanglement. However, these requirements could significantly increase the time and cost in data collection and limit the applicability of these methods when such data are not available. Moreover, these methods generally do not guarantee disentanglement. In this paper, we present a novel framework that learns theoretically and practically superior disentanglement from *single* modality magnetic resonance images. Moreover, we propose a new information-based metric to quantitatively evaluate disentanglement. Comparisons over existing disentangling methods demonstrate that the proposed method achieves superior performance in disentanglement and cross-domain image-to-image translation tasks.

Keywords: Disentangle · Harmonization · Domain adaptation

1 Introduction

The recent development of disentangled representation learning benefits various medical image analysis tasks including segmentation [17,21,24], quality assessment [12], domain adaptation [25], and image-to-image translation (I2I) [10,29]. The underlying assumption of disentanglement is that a high-dimensional observation x is generated by a latent variable z, where z can be decomposed into independent factors with each factor capturing a certain type of variation of x, i.e., the probability density functions satisfy $p(z_1, z_2) = p(z_1)p(z_2)$ and $z = (z_1, z_2)$ [20]. For medical images, it is commonly assumed that z is

Supplementary Information The online version contains supplementary material available at https://doi.org/10.1007/978-3-031-17027-0_6.

a composition of contrast (i.e., acquisition-related) and anatomical information of image x [7,10,18,21,29]. While the contrast representations capture specific information about the imaging modality, acquisition parameters, and cohort, the anatomical representations are generally assumed to be invariant to image domains. Here we assume that images acquired from the same scanner with the same acquisition parameters are from the same domain. It has been shown that the disentangled domain-invariant anatomical representation is a robust input for segmentation [7,17,21], and the contrast representation provides information about image acquisitions. Recombining the anatomical representation with the desired contrast representation also enables cross-domain I2I [21,29].

Disentangling anatomy and contrast in medical images is a nontrivial task. Locatello et al. [19] showed that it is theoretically impossible to learn disentangled representations from independent and identically distributed observations without inductive bias (e.g., domain labels or paired data). Accordingly, most research efforts have focused on learning disentangled representations with image pairs or auxiliary labels. Specifically, image pairs introduce an inductive bias that the two images differ exactly in one factor of z and share the remaining information. Multi-contrast or multi-scanner images of the same subject are the most commonly used paired data. For example, T_1-weighted (T_1-w)/T_2-weighted (T_2-w) magnetic resonance (MR) images [10,21,28], MR/computational tomography images [7], or multi-scanner images [17,18] of the same subject are often used in disentangling contrast and anatomy. The underlying assumption is that the paired images share the same anatomy (domain-invariant) while differing in image contrast (domain-specific). The requirement of paired training images with the same anatomy is a limitation due to the extra time and cost of data collection. Even though such paired data are available in some applications—for example, paired T_1-w and T_2-w images are routinely acquired in MR imaging—registration error, artifacts, and difference in resolution could violate the fundamental assumption that only one factor of z changes between the pairs. As we show in Sect. 3, non-ideal paired data can have negative effects in disentangling.

Labels, such as manual delineations or domain labels, usually provide explicit supervision in either the disentangled representations or synthetic images generated by the I2I algorithm for capturing desired properties. [7,8] used manual delineations to guide the disentangled anatomical representations to be binary masks of the human heart. In [14,16], researchers used domain labels with domain-specific image discriminators and a cycle consistency loss to encourage the synthetic images to be in the correct domain and the representations to be properly disentangled. Although these methods have shown encouraging performance in I2I tasks, there is still potential for improvements. The dependency of pixel-level annotations or domain labels limits the applicability, since these labels are sometimes unavailable or inaccurate. Additionally, the cycle consistency loss is generally memory consuming and found to be an over-strict constraint of I2I [3], which leads to limited scalability when there are many image domains.

Can we overcome the limitations of current disentangling methods and design a model that **does not rely on paired multi-modal images or labels** and is also scalable in a large number of image domains? Deviating from most existing

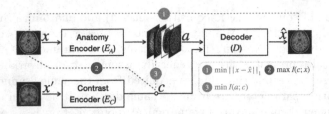

Fig. 1. The proposed disentangling framework has an encoder-decoder like structure. x and x' are two slices from different orientations of the same 3D volume, which we assume embed the same contrast but different anatomy information. $I(\cdot;\cdot)$ denotes MI.

literature that heavily relies on paired multi-modal images for training, we propose a **single modality disentangling framework.** Instead of using domain-specific image discriminators or cycle consistency losses, we design a novel distribution discriminator that is shared by all image domains for **theoretically and practically superior disentanglement** $p(z_1, z_2) = p(z_1)p(z_2)$. Additionally, we present **an information-based metric to quantitatively measure disentanglement.** We demonstrate the broad applicability of the proposed method in a multi-site brain MR image harmonization task and a cardiac MR image segmentation task. Results show that our single-modal disentangling framework achieves performance comparable to methods which rely on multi-modal images for disentanglement. Furthermore, we demonstrate that the proposed framework can be incorporated into existing methods and trained with a mixture of paired and single modality data to further improve performance.

2   Method

2.1   The Single-Modal Disentangling Network

General Framework. As shown in Fig. 1, the proposed method has an autoencoder-like structure. The inputs x and x' are two slices from different orientations of the same 3D volume. x and x' introduce an inductive bias that they have the same contrast but different anatomy information. $I(\cdot;\cdot)$ denotes mutual information (MI). Note that the proposed method can be applied to datasets of other organs, as shown in Sect. 3; we use brain MR images for demonstration purposes. The anatomy encoder has a U-Net [23] structure similar to [7,10,17]. It generates one-hot encoded anatomical representations $a \in \mathbb{R}^{H \times W \times M}$, where H and W are with the same spatial dimension of x, and M is the number of channels. The contrast encoder is composed of a sequence of convolutional blocks with output contrast representations $c \in \mathbb{R}^2$. c is then broadcast to $H \times W \times 2$ and concatenated with a as the input to the decoder, which is also a U-Net. The same networks are shared by all image domains, so the model size stays constant.

   The overall objectives of the framework are 1) to disentangle anatomical and contrast information from input images without multi-modal paired data or labels and 2) to generate high quality synthetic images based on the disentangled representations. The above two objectives can be mathematically summarized into three terms (also shown in Fig. 1) that we show are optimizable by loss functions, $\mathcal{L} \triangleq \lambda_1 \|x - \hat{x}\|_1 - \lambda_2 I(c; x) + \lambda_3 I(a; c)$, where λ's are the hyperparameters and $\|x - \hat{x}\|_1$ is the l_1 reconstruction loss that encourages the generated image $\hat{x}$ to be similar to the original image x. The second term $-I(c; x)$ encourages c to capture as much information of x as possible. Since c is calculated from x' instead of x with $E_C(\cdot)$ and the shared information between x' and x is the contrast, maximizing $I(c; x)$ guides $E_C(\cdot)$ to extract contrast information. Lastly, minimizing $I(a; c)$ penalizes a and c from capturing common information, thus encouraging disentanglement. Since c captures contrast information by maximizing $I(c; x)$, this helps the anatomy encoder $E_A(\cdot)$ learn anatomical information from the input x. This can also prevent a trivial solution where $E_A(\cdot)$ and $D(\cdot)$ learn an identity transformation. In the next section, we show how the two MI terms are optimized in training. We also theoretically show that a and c are perfectly disentangled, i.e., $I(a; c) = 0$, at the global minimum of $E_A(\cdot)$.

Maximizing. $I(c; x)$ We adopt DeepInfomax [13] to maximize the lower bound of $I(c; x)$ during training. This approach uses this inequality:

$$I(c; x) \geq \hat{I}(c; x) \triangleq \mathbb{E}_{p(c,x)} \left[-\text{sp} \left(-T(c, x) \right) \right] - \mathbb{E}_{p(c)p(x)} \left[\text{sp} \left(T(c, x) \right) \right], \quad (1)$$

where $\text{sp}(r) = \log(1 + e^r)$ is the softplus function and $T(\cdot, \cdot)$ is a trainable auxiliary network $T(c, x): \mathcal{C} \times \mathcal{X} \rightarrow \mathbb{R}$. The gradient calculated by maximizing Eq. (1) is applied to both $T(\cdot, \cdot)$ and $E_C(\cdot)$. Density functions $p(c, x)$ and $p(c)p(x)$ are sampled by selecting matched pairs $\{(c^{(i)}, x^{(i)})\}_{i=1}^N$ and shuffled pairs $\{(c^{(i)}, x^{(l_i)})\}_{i=1}^N$ from a mini-batch with N being the batch size and $c = E_C(x')$. Note that paired multi-modal images are not required; x and x' are 2D slices from the same volume with different orientations. i is the instance index of a mini-batch and $\{l_i\}_{i=1}^N$ is a permutation of sequence $\{1, \ldots, N\}$.

Minimizing. $I(a; c)$ Since Eq. (1) provides a lower bound of MI, it cannot be used to minimize $I(a; c)$. We propose a novel way to *minimize* $I(a; c)$. Inspired by the distribution matching property of generative adversarial networks (GANs) [11], we introduce a distribution discriminator $U(\cdot, \cdot): \mathcal{A} \times \mathcal{C} \rightarrow \mathbb{R}$ that distinguishes whether the inputs (a, c) are sampled from the joint distribution $p(a, c)$ or product of the marginals $p(a)p(c)$. Note that c is detached from the computational graph while minimizing $I(a; c)$, so the GAN loss only affects $U(a, c)$ and $E_A(x)$, where $E_A(x)$ tries to "fool" $U(a, c)$ by generating anatomical representations a, such that $p(a, c)$ and $p(a)p(c)$ are sufficiently indistinguishable.

Theorem 1. $E_A(x)$ *achieves global minimum* $\iff p(a, c) = p(a)p(c)$.

Theorem 1 says a and c are disentangled at the global minimum of $E_A(x)$. The minmax training objective between $E_A(x)$ and $U(a, c)$ is given by

$$\min_{E_A} \max_{U} \mathbb{E}_{p(a,c)} \left[\log U(a, c) \right] + \mathbb{E}_{p(a)p(c)} \left[\log \left(1 - U(a, c) \right) \right], \quad (2)$$

where $a = E_A(x)$. Densities $p(a, c)$ and $p(a)p(c)$ are sampled by randomly selecting matched pairs $\{(a^{(i)}, c^{(i)})\}_{i=1}^N$ and shuffled pairs $\{(a^{(i)}, c^{(l_i)})\}_{i=1}^N$, respectively.

Implementation Details. There are in total five networks shared by all domains. $E_A(\cdot)$ and $D(\cdot)$ are both U-Nets with all convolutional layers being a kernel size of 3×3 convolution followed by instance normalization and LeakyReLU. $E_C(\cdot)$ is a five-layer CNN with 4×4 convolutions with stride 2. The kernel size of the last layer equals the spatial dimension of the features, making the output variable c a two-channel feature with $H = W = 1$. Both $T(\cdot, \cdot)$ and $U(\cdot, \cdot)$ are five-layer CNNs. We use the Adam optimizer in all our experiments, where our model consumed approximately 20GB GPU memory for training with batch size 16 and image dimension 288×288. Our learning rate is 10^{-4}, $\lambda_1 = 1.0$, and $\lambda_2 = \lambda_3 = 0.1$. Our code is available from https://iacl.ece.jhu.edu/index.php?title=Resources.

2.2   A New Metric to Evaluate Disentanglement

Since MI between two perfectly disentangled variables is zero, intuition would have us directly estimate MI between two latent variables to evaluate disentanglement. MINE [4] provides an efficient way to estimate MI using a neural network. However, simply measuring MI is less informative since MI is not upper bounded; e.g., how much worse is $I(a; c) = 10$ compared with $I(a; c) = 0.1$? Inspired by the fact that $I(a; c) = H(c) - H(c|a)$, where $H(\cdot)$ is entropy, we define a bounded ratio $R_I(a; c) \triangleq I(a; c)/H(c) \in [0, 1]$ to evaluate disentanglement. $R_I(a, c)$ has a nice theoretical interpretation: the *proportion* of information that c shares with a. Different from MIG [9], which requires the ground truth factor of variations, the ratio $R_I(a; c)$ directly estimates how well the two latent variables are disentangled.

When the distribution $p(c)$ is known, $H(c)$ can be directly calculated using the definition $H(c) = -\sum p(c) \log p(c)$. To estimate $H(c)$ when $p(c)$ is an arbitrary distribution, we follow [6]. Accordingly, $R_I(a; c)$ for unknown $p(c)$ is given by

$$R_I(a; c) \triangleq \frac{I(a; c)}{H(c)} = \frac{\mathcal{D}_{\mathrm{KL}}\left[p(a, c) \| p(a) p(c)\right]}{-\mathbb{E}_{p(c)}\left[\log q(c)\right] - \mathcal{D}_{\mathrm{KL}}\left[p(c) \| q(z)\right]}, \tag{3}$$

where $z \sim q(z) = \mathcal{N}(0, \mathbb{I})$ is an auxiliary variable with the same dimension as c. The two Kullback-Leibler divergence terms can be estimated using MINE [4]. The cross-entropy term is approximated by the empirical mean $-\frac{1}{N} \sum_{i=1}^N \log q(c_i)$.

3   Experiments and Results

We evaluate the proposed single-modal disentangling framework on two different tasks: harmonizing multi-site brain MR images and domain adaptation (DA) for cardiac image segmentation. In the brain MR harmonization experiment, we also quantitatively evaluate disentanglement of different comparison methods.

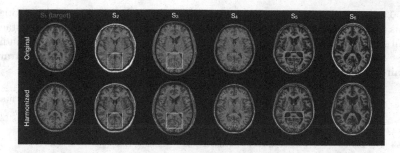

Fig. 2. T_1-w brain MR images from ten sites (S_1 to S_{10}) are harmonized to S_1. Six representative sites are shown. Green boxes highlight gray and white matter contrasts becoming more similar to the target after harmonization. Yellow boxes indicate harmonization error from the proposed method. (Color figure online)

Brain MR Harmonization. T_1-w and T_2-w MR images of the human brain collected at ten different sites (denoted as S_1 to S_{10}) are used in our harmonization task. We use the datasets [1,15,22] and preprocessing reported in [29]. For each site, 10 and 5 subjects were used for training and validation, respectively. As shown in Fig. 2, the original T_1-w images have different contrasts due to their acquisition parameters. We seek a T_1-w harmonization such that the image contrast of the source site matches the target site while maintaining the underlying anatomy. We have a set of held-out subjects ($N = 10$) who traveled between S_1 and S_2 to evaluate harmonization.

Compare with unpaired I2I method without disentangling. We first compared our method trained only on T_1-w images (100%U) with CycleGAN [27], which conducts unpaired I2I based on image discriminators and a cycle consistency loss without disentanglement. Results in Table 1 show that our (100%U) outperforms CycleGAN with statistical significance ($p < 0.01$) in a paired Wilcoxon signed rank test, where the null hypothesis is that the SSIM or PSNR difference between two comparison methods has zero median.

Does single-modal disentangling perform as well as multi-modal disentangling? We then compared our method with two different disentangling methods which use paired T_1-w and T_2-w for training. Specifically, Adeli et al. [2] learns latent representations that are mean independent of a protected variable. In our application, a and c are the latent and protected variable, respectively. Zuo et al. [29] tackles the harmonization problem with disentangled representations without explicitly minimizing $I(a; c)$. Our method, which was only trained on unpaired data (100%U), has similar performance with Adeli et al. [2] and Zuo et al. [29], both of which rely on paired T_1-w and T_2-w images for training (see Table 1). Unfortunately, we do not have enough data for a statistical statement.

Are paired data helpful to our method? We present three ablations of our method: training with all T_1-w images (100%U), training with 50% paired and 50% unpaired images (50%P, 50%U), and training with 100% paired T_1-w and T_2-w images (100%P). The existence of paired T_1-w and T_2-w images of the same

Table 1. Numerical comparisons between the proposed approach and existing I2I methods in a harmonization task. SSIM and PSNR are calculated in 3D by stacking 2D axial slices and are reported as "mean ± standard deviation". Bold numbers indicate the best mean performance. U: training with unpaired data (T_1-w only). P: training with paired T_1-w and T_2-w images.

	Training data	I2I: S_1 to S_2		I2I: S_2 to S_1		Disentangle
		SSIM (%)	PSNR (dB)	SSIM (%)	PSNR (dB)	$R_I(a; c)$ (%)
Before I2I	–	87.54 ± 1.18	26.68 ± 0.77	87.54 ± 1.18	26.68 ± 0.77	–
CycleGAN [27]	100%U	89.62 ± 1.14	27.35 ± 0.52	90.23 ± 1.12	28.15 ± 0.59	–
Adeli [2]	100%P	89.92 ± 0.98	27.47 ± 0.52	90.36 ± 1.05	28.41 ± 0.49	5.9
Zuo [29]	100%P	90.63 ± 1.08	27.60 ± 0.61	90.89 ± 1.01	28.14 ± 0.54	10.8
Ours	100%U	90.25 ± 1.02	27.86 ± 0.59	90.52 ± 1.03	28.23 ± 0.45	**0.1**
Ours	50%U, 50%P	$\mathbf{90.96 \pm 1.00}$	$\mathbf{28.55 \pm 0.61}$	$\mathbf{91.16 \pm 1.31}$	$\mathbf{28.60 \pm 0.49}$	1.5
Ours	100%P	90.27 ± 0.95	27.88 ± 0.54	90.70 ± 1.02	28.59 ± 0.52	3.1

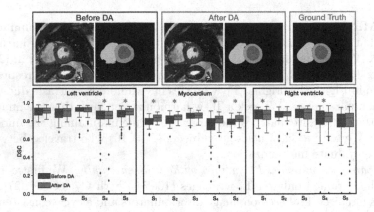

Fig. 3. Top: An example of improved segmentation from S_4 after DA. Bottom: DSC of multi-site cardiac image segmentation. The segmentation model was trained on S_1 to S_3, and then applied to a held-out dataset with images from all five sites. DA was conducted to translate all images to S_3 using the proposed method. Asterisks indicate statistically significant tests.

anatomy provides an extra constraint: a of T_1-w and T_2-w should be identical. We observe in Tabel 1 that introducing a small amount of paired multi-modal images in training can boost the performance of our method, as our (50%U, 50%P) achieves the best performance. Yet, training the proposed method using all paired images has no benefit to harmonization, which we discuss in Sect. 4.

Do we learn better disentanglement? We calculated the proposed $R_I(a; c)$ to evaluate all the comparison methods that learn disentangled representations. Results are shown in the last column of Table 1. All three ablations of the proposed method achieve superior disentangling performance than the other methods. Out of the five comparisons, Zuo et al. [29] has the worst disentanglement between a and c; this is likely because Zuo et al. only encourages disentangling between a and domain labels. Surprisingly, a and c become more entangled as we introduce more T_2-w images in training. A possible reason could be that T_1-w and T_2-w images carry slightly different observable anatomical information, making it impossible to completely disentangle anatomy and contrast because several factors of z are changing simultaneously. A similar effect is also reported in [26], where non-ideal paired data are used in disentangling.

Cardiac MR Image Segmentation. To further evaluate the proposed method, we used data from the M&M cardiac segmentation challenge [5], where cine MR images of the human heart were collected by six sites, out of which five (S_1 to S_5) are available to us. The task is to segment the left and right ventricle and the left ventricular myocardium of the human heart. We followed the challenge guidelines to split data so that the training data (MR images and manual delineations) only include S_1, S_2, and S_3, and the validation and testing data include all five sites. In this way there is a domain shift between the training sites (S_1 thru S_3) and testing sites (S_4 and S_5). Since images from all five sites are available to challenge participants, DA can be applied. Due to the absence of paired data, we only applied the proposed 100%U to this task (other evaluated disentangling methods in the brain MR harmonization task cannot be applied here).

Does our method alleviate domain shift in downstream segmentation? We adopted a 2D U-Net structure similar to the B_1 model reported in [5] as our segmentation baseline. Without DA, our baseline method achieved a performance in Dice similarity coefficient (DSC) within the top 5. Due to domain shift, the baseline method has a decreased performance on S_4 and S_5 (see Fig. 3). We applied the proposed method trained on MR images from all five available sites to translate testing MR images to site S_3 (as the baseline segmentation model has the best overall performance on the original S_3 images). Due to the poor through-plane resolution of cine MR images, we chose x and x' by selecting slices from two different cine time frames. Segmentation performance was re-evaluated using images after DA. Paired Wilcoxon test on each label of each site shows that the segmentation model has significantly improved ($p < 0.01$) DSC for all labels of S_4 and S_5 after DA, except for the right ventricle of S_5. Although segmentation is improved after DA, the ability of our method to alleviate domain shift is not unlimited; the segmentation performance on S_4 and S_5 is still worse than the training sites. We regard this as a limitation for future improvement.

4 Discussion and Conclusion

We present a single-modal MR disentangling framework with theoretical guarantees and an information-based metric for evaluating disentanglement. We showcase the broad applicability of our method in brain MR harmonization and DA for cardiac image segmentation. We show in the harmonization task that satisfactory performance can be achieved without paired data. With limited paired data for training, our method demonstrates superior performance over existing methods. However, with all paired data for training, we observed decreased performance in both harmonization and disentanglement. We view this seemingly surprising observation as a result of the disentanglement-reconstruction trade-off reported in [26]. This is also a reminder for future research: using paired multi-modal images for disentangling may have negative effects when the paired data are non-ideal. Our cardiac segmentation experiment shows that domain shift can be reduced with the proposed method.

Acknowledgement. The authors thank BLSA participants. This work was supported in part by the Intramural Research Program of the NIH, National Institute on Aging, in part by the NINDS grants R01-NS082347 (PI: P. A. Calabresi) and U01-NS111678 (PI: P. A. Calabresi), and in part by the TREAT-MS study funded by the Patient-Centered Outcomes Research Institute (PCORI/MS-1610-37115).

References

1. IXI Brain Development Dataset. https://brain-development.org/ixi-dataset/
2. Adeli, E., et al.: Representation learning with statistical independence to mitigate bias. In: Proceedings of the IEEE/CVF Winter Conference on Applications of Computer Vision, pp. 2513–2523 (2021)
3. Amodio, M., Krishnaswamy, S.: Travelgan: image-to-image translation by transformation vector learning. In: Proceedings of the IEEE/CVF Conference on Computer Vision and Pattern Recognition, pp. 8983–8992 (2019)
4. Belghazi, M.I., et al.: MINE: Mutual Information Neural Estimation. arXiv preprint arXiv:1801.04062 (2018)
5. Campello, V.M., et al.: Multi-centre, multi-vendor and multi-disease cardiac segmentation: the M&Ms challenge. IEEE Trans. Med. Imag. **40**(12), 3543–3554 (2021)
6. Chan, C., Al-Bashabsheh, A., Huang, H.P., Lim, M., Tam, D.S.H., Zhao, C.: Neural Entropic Estimation: A Faster Path to Mutual Information Estimation. arXiv preprint arXiv:1905.12957 (2019)
7. Chartsias, A., et al.: Disentangled representation learning in cardiac image analysis. Med. Image Anal. **58**, 101535 (2019)
8. Chen, C., Dou, Q., Chen, H., Qin, J., Heng, P.A.: Synergistic image and feature adaptation: towards cross-modality domain adaptation for medical image segmentation. In: Proceedings of the AAAI Conference on Artificial Intelligence, vol. 33, pp. 865–872 (2019)
9. Chen, R.T., Li, X., Grosse, R.B., Duvenaud, D.K.: Isolating sources of disentanglement in variational autoencoders. Adv. Neural Inf. Process. Syst. **31** (2018)
10. Dewey, B.E., et al.: A disentangled latent space for cross-site MRI harmonization. In: Martel, A.L., et al. (eds.) MICCAI 2020. LNCS, vol. 12267, pp. 720–729. Springer, Cham (2020). https://doi.org/10.1007/978-3-030-59728-3_70
11. Goodfellow, I., et al.: Generative adversarial nets. Adv. Neural Inf. Process. Syst. **27** (2014)
12. Hays, S.P., Zuo, L., Carass, A., Prince, J.: Evaluating the impact of MR image contrast on whole brain segmentation. In: Medical Imaging 2022: Image Processing, vol. 12032, pp. 122–126. SPIE (2022)
13. Hjelm, R.D., et al.: Learning Deep Representations by Mutual Information Estimation and Maximization. arXiv preprint arXiv:1808.06670 (2018)

14. Huang, X., Liu, M.Y., Belongie, S., Kautz, J.: Multimodal unsupervised image-to-image translation. In: Proceedings of the European Conference on Computer Vision, pp. 172–189 (2018)
15. LaMontagne, P.J., et al.: OASIS-3: Longitudinal Neuroimaging, Clinical, and Cognitive Dataset for Normal Aging and Alzheimer Disease. MedRxiv (2019)
16. Lee, H.Y., et al.: Drit++: diverse image-to-image translation via disentangled representations. Int. J. Comput. Vis. **128**(10), 2402–2417 (2020)
17. Liu, Y., et al.: Variational intensity cross channel encoder for unsupervised vessel segmentation on OCT angiography. In: Medical Imaging 2020: Image Processing, vol. 11313, p. 113130Y. International Society for Optics and Photonics (2020)
18. Liu, Y., et al.: Disentangled representation learning for octa vessel segmentation with limited training data. IEEE Trans. Med. Imag. (2022)
19. Locatello, F., et al.: Challenging common assumptions in the unsupervised learning of disentangled representations. In: International Conference on Machine Learning, pp. 4114–4124. PMLR (2019)
20. Locatello, F., Poole, B., Rätsch, G., Schölkopf, B., Bachem, O., Tschannen, M.: Weakly-supervised disentanglement without compromises. In: International Conference on Machine Learning, pp. 6348–6359. PMLR (2020)
21. Ouyang, J., Adeli, E., Pohl, K.M., Zhao, Q., Zaharchuk, G.: Representation disentanglement for multi-modal brain MRI analysis. In: Feragen, A., Sommer, S., Schnabel, J., Nielsen, M. (eds.) IPMI 2021. LNCS, vol. 12729, pp. 321–333. Springer, Cham (2021). https://doi.org/10.1007/978-3-030-78191-0_25
22. Resnick, S.M., et al.: One-year age changes in MRI brain volumes in older adults. Cerebral Cortex **10**(5), 464–472 (2000)
23. Ronneberger, O., Fischer, P., Brox, T.: U-Net: convolutional networks for biomedical image segmentation. In: Navab, N., Hornegger, J., Wells, W.M., Frangi, A.F. (eds.) MICCAI 2015. LNCS, vol. 9351, pp. 234–241. Springer, Cham (2015). https://doi.org/10.1007/978-3-319-24574-4_28
24. Shao, M., Zuo, L., Carass, A., Zhuo, J., Gullapalli, R.P., Prince, J.L.: Evaluating the impact of MR image harmonization on thalamus deep network segmentation. In: Proceedings of SPIE Medical Imaging (SPIE-MI 2022), San Diego, CA, 20–24 February 2022, vol. 12032, pp. 115–121 (2021)
25. Tang, Y., Tang, Y., Zhu, Y., Xiao, J., Summers, R.M.: A disentangled generative model for disease decomposition in chest X-rays via normal image synthesis. Med. Image Anal. **67**, 101839 (2021)
26. Träuble, F., et al.: On disentangled representations learned from correlated data. In: International Conference on Machine Learning, pp. 10401–10412. PMLR (2021)
27. Zhu, J.Y., Park, T., Isola, P., Efros, A.A.: Unpaired image-to-image translation using cycle-consistent adversarial networks. In: Proceedings of the IEEE International Conference on Computer Vision, pp. 2223–2232 (2017)
28. Zuo, L., et al.: Information-based disentangled representation learning for unsupervised MR harmonization. In: Feragen, A., Sommer, S., Schnabel, J., Nielsen, M. (eds.) IPMI 2021. LNCS, vol. 12729, pp. 346–359. Springer, Cham (2021). https://doi.org/10.1007/978-3-030-78191-0_27
29. Zuo, L., et al.: Unsupervised MR harmonization by learning disentangled representations using information Bottleneck theory. NeuroImage **243**, 118569 (2021)

CTooth+: A Large-Scale Dental Cone Beam Computed Tomography Dataset and Benchmark for Tooth Volume Segmentation

Weiwei Cui[2], Yaqi Wang[1(✉)], Yilong Li[2], Dan Song[4], Xingyong Zuo[4],
Jiaojiao Wang[1], Yifan Zhang[3], Huiyu Zhou[5], Bung san Chong[2],
Liaoyuan Zeng[4], and Qianni Zhang[2(✉)]

[1] Communication University of Zhejiang, Hangzhou, China
wangyaqi@cuz.edu.cn
[2] Queen Mary University of London, London, UK
[3] West China Hospital of Stomatology, Sichuan University, Chengdu, China
[4] University of Electronic Science and Technology of China, Chengdu, China
[5] University of Leicester, Leicester, UK

Abstract. Accurate tooth volume segmentation is a prerequisite for computer-aided dental analysis. Deep learning-based tooth segmentation methods have achieved satisfying performances but require a large quantity of tooth data with ground truth. The dental data publicly available is limited meaning the existing methods can not be reproduced, evaluated and applied in clinical practice. In this paper, we establish a 3D dental CBCT dataset CTooth+, with 22 fully annotated volumes and 146 unlabeled volumes. We further evaluate several state-of-the-art tooth volume segmentation strategies based on fully-supervised learning, semi-supervised learning and active learning, and define the performance principles. This work provides a new benchmark for the tooth volume segmentation task, and the experiment can serve as the baseline for future AI-based dental imaging research and clinical application development. The codebase and dataset are released here.

Keywords: 3D segmentation · Dental dataset · Fully supervised learning · Semi-supervised learning · Active learning

1 Introduction

Accurately segmented tooth volumes provide valuable 3D information for the clinical diagnosis such as root shape, curvature, tooth size, the spatial relationship of multiple teeth. However, manually delineating all tooth regions is labour-consuming, error-prone and expensive.

Some learning-based methods have been proposed to automatically segment tooth regions and achieve approving results. Several shallow learning-based methods try to quickly segment teeth from X-ray or CBCT images such as region-based [16], threshold-based [2], and cluster-based [3] approaches. Recently, deep

H. V. Nguyen et al. (Eds.): DALI 2022, LNCS 13567, pp. 64–73, 2022.
https://doi.org/10.1007/978-3-031-17027-0_7

learning-based methods attempt to solve 3D tooth segmentation. Mask R-CNN is applied on tooth segmentation and detection [8]. Modified 3D Unet structures are well-designed with initial dental masks or complex backbones [25]. However, these methods are mostly evaluated on small or in-house datasets. It is still hard to reproduce these segmentation performances as the dental dataset and code are not published.

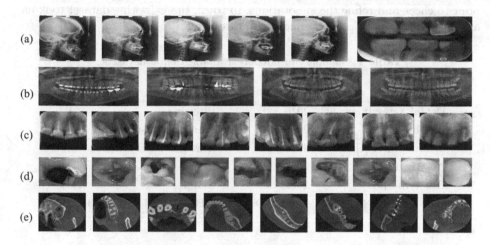

Fig. 1. A few samples from different publicly available dental image datasets are illustrated. (a) Dental X-ray Image, (b) LNDb, (c) AGMB, (d) Teeth_dataset, and (e) CTooth+.

We review several dental image datasets and summarise their contributions. Seven types of tooth structures are marked on Dental X-ray Image dataset [23]. LNDb dataset contains polygon boundary annotations of teeth on X-ray images [21]. AGMB evaluates root canal therapy on RGB images [14]. Teeth_dataset is proposed for caries classification [1]. Some samples of these existing datasets are shown in Fig. 1. To our knowledge, no 3D dental CBCT dataset has ever been published for open-access in the medical image processing domain.

Our work is the first comprehensive study on 3D dental data collection, annotation and evaluation. We publish a 3D dataset CTooth+ and release tooth segmentation performances based on fully-supervised learning, semi-supervised learning and active learning methods. CTooth+ dataset provides a research fundamental for following-up automatic dental segmentation studies.

2   CTooth+ Dataset

2.1   Dataset Summary

The main properties of the existing 2D and 3D dental datasets are summarized in Table 1. Compared with the published dental datasets, most of the existing datasets contain only 2D images from various tooth imaging modalities and the amount of data is relative small. Our CTooth+ fully maintains the three-dimensional characteristics of teeth, and the number of data samples exceeds 30k slices, far exceeding the existing 2D dental datasets. The data set consists of 5504 annotated CBCT images of 22 patients and 25876 unlabeled images of 146 patients. All patient information is coded for the purpose of protecting privacy. For each volume, we roughly spent 6 h to annotate tooth regions and 1 more hour to check and refine the annotations. In total, the CTooth+ dataset took us around 10 months to collect, annotate and review.

Table 1. Summary of publicly available dental datasets.

Dataset	Year	Modality	Type	Scan
Dental X-ray Image [23]	2015	2D	Bitewing	120
LNDb [21]	2016	2D	Panomatic X-ray	1,500
Teeth_dataset [1]	2020	2D	Intraoral RGB image	77
AGMB [14]	2021	2D	Root canal image	245
Our CTooth [7]	2022	3D	CBCT	7,368
Our CTooth+	**2022**	**3D**	**CBCT**	**31,380**

The images in CTooth+ were acquired with a OP300, manufactured by Instrumentarium Orthopantomograph®. CBCT slices were acquired in the DICOM format at the University of Electronic Science and Technology of China hospital. All CBCT slices were scanned before dental operations, with a resolution of 266 × 266 pixels in the axial view. The in-plane resolution is about $0.25 \times 0.25 \, mm^2$ and the slice thickness range from 0.25 mm to 0.3 mm.

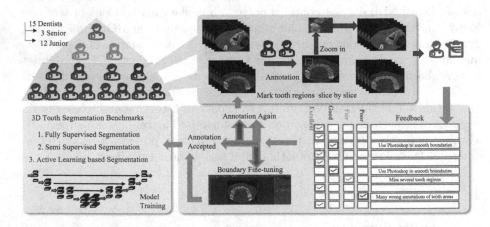

Fig. 2. Dataset annotation and quality control procedure.

2.2 Expert Annotation and Quality Assessment

Figure 2 illustrates the whole procedure for CTooth+ dataset annotation and quality control procedure. Scans were annotated by 15 dentists. Twelve junior dentists with at least two years of experience manually marked all teeth regions. They first used ITKSNAP [27] to delineate tooth regions slice-by-slice in the axial view. Then the annotations were modified according to the coronal view and sagittal view.

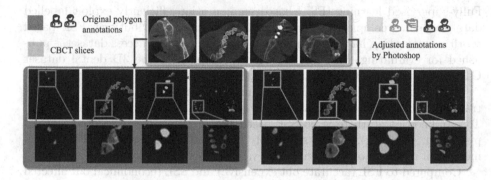

Fig. 3. Annotation adjustment.

Three senior experts with at least ten years of experience were invited to evaluate the tooth annotations. The senior experts assessed the annotation quality, and marked a quality level (excellent, good, fail and poor) on each tooth annotation. "Excellent" annotations were stored in the CTooth+ dataset directly. "Good" annotations were fed into Phototshop software [17] for fine-tuning according to the experts' feedback. "Fair" and "Poor" annotations and their feedback were put back into the unlabelled data pool and were marked again. In Fig. 3, we illustrate a set of "Good" annotations before and after adjustment. It is clear that the tooth boundaries are more precise and smoother after necessary adjustment.

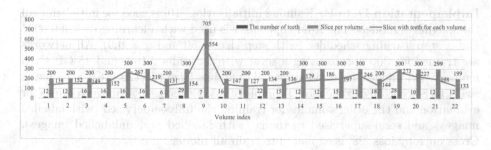

Fig. 4. Annotation statistics of CTooth+.

Statistics of annotated teeth are illustrated in Fig. 4. All image volumes have about 12 teeth, 200 or 300 slices, and 150 slices with teeth except for the 9th volume. The unlabelled images have similar statistics as the annotated images. The similar data statistics attributes ensure the stability of model training. In addition, variance in tooth shape, restorations, implants inside each volume forces the segmentation model to learn with robustness and generalizability.

2.3   Potential Research Topics

Fully-supervised learning (FSL) based segmentation efficiently exploit labelled data and solve complex challenges, e.g. imbalanced distributions. FSL based tooth segmentation has been studied recently but no open-access dataset is published for evaluating these methods. Here, we propose the 3D dental dataset CTooth+ and reproduce eight FSL segmentation methods based on it.

Semi-supervised learning (SSL) requires less expert annotations for model training, relieving the time and labour burden associated to data annotation. To our knowledge, there is no SSL-based tooth volume segmentation method published. This work attempts to apply four state-of-the-art SSL medical segmentation methods on CTooth+ and evaluate their performances.

Compared to FSL (accurate but expensive) and SSL (economical but affected by noise), various active learning (AL) strategies are designed to enlarge the training set by iteratively selecting informative samples. In this paper, we extend six active learning methods to their 3D version and evaluate their tooth segmentation performances on CTooth+.

3   Experiments and Results

3.1   Evaluation Metrics and Implementations on the CTooth+

Evaluation Metrics: The segmentation results are evaluated using dice similarity coefficient (DSC), intersection-over-union (IOU), sensitivity (SEN), positive predictive value (ppv), Hausdorff distance (HD), average symmetric surface distance (ASSD), surface overlap (SO), and surface dice (SD) [7].

Implementation Details: Kaiming initialization [10] is used for initializing all the weights of models. The Adam optimizer is used with a learning rate of 0.0004 and a step learning scheduler (with step size = 50 and $\gamma = 0.9$). All networks are trained for 300 epochs using a sever with 2 Nvidia A100s and 48 GB CPU memory. All images are divided into 3D patches (size (64,128,128)) with batch size 4 to 8 according to the model complexity. We choose 20% image volumes for evaluation and the other volumes for training the fully-supervised (with labelled images) and semi-supervised methods (with labelled and unlabelled images). Cross entropy loss [28] is exploited to train all models.

3.2   Benchmark for Fully-Supervised Tooth Volume Segmentation

We present the 3D FSL tooth segmentation performances on 8 fully-supervised segmentation methods. In Table 2, Attention Unet [19] outperforms other methods in most metrics including DSC 86.60%, IOU 76.45% and PPV 87.79%, ASSD 0.27 mm, respectively. Hausdorff distance on nnUnet [12] is minimal at 1.29 mm, and the sensitivity metric on Voxresnet [26] achieves the best. DenseUnet [9] has a satisfying results on the accuracy of tooth surface (SO and SD). However, we observe that 3D SkipDenseNet [4] and DenseVoxelNet [26] are both inefficient for segmenting 3D tooth volumes since their network structures are deeper than others causing network overfitting on CToooth+.

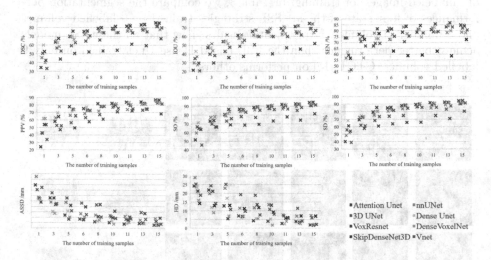

Fig. 5. Evaluations on segmentation when changing the amount of training volumes.

Table 2. Evaluation comparison among differnet tooth volume segmentation methods trained on 17 volumes.

Method	DSC	IOU	SEN	PPV	HD	ASSD	SO	SD
3D SkipDenseNet [4]	64.99	49.16	73.54	69.49	7.61	1.08	80.17	76.40
DenseVoxelNet [26]	76.45	62.22	83.16	75.36	5.10	0.62	89.54	88.76
3D Unet [6]	79.51	66.40	78.21	82.78	8.02	1.01	89.22	88.76
VNet [18]	81.21	68.58	80.88	83.27	1.61	0.29	93.11	92.90
Voxresnet [26]	85.07	74.25	86.58	84.29	5.14	0.45	94.11	94.04
nnUnet [12]	85.48	74.83	84.56	87.22	**1.29**	**0.27**	95.09	95.03
Dense Unet [9]	86.27	76.11	**90.80**	83.23	2.08	0.39	**95.98**	**95.91**
Attention Unet [19]	**86.60**	**76.45**	86.11	**87.79**	1.72	**0.27**	95.25	95.20

We further perform an ablation study on the FSL tooth segmentation task. Figure 5 shows the quantitative segmentation performances among the FSL segmentation methods when changing the number of training sample volumes. It is clear that all performance metrics increase when the number of data samples increases evenly. However, noise and uneven data sampling make the increase in data volume unproportional to the performance gain. Hence, more designs are considered to increase network robustness and reduce the noise effect.

3.3 Benchmark for Semi-supervised Tooth Volume Segmentation

SSL based tooth segmentation exploits less ground truth and a large number of unlabeled images for training. In Table 3, we compare the segmentation performances of four state-of-the-art SSL strategies trained by 9 labelled volumes and 8 unlabelled volumes. Experimental results show that all these SSL models achieve better performance than the FSL based Dense Unet trained on only 9 labelled volumes. CTCT [15] outperforms others.

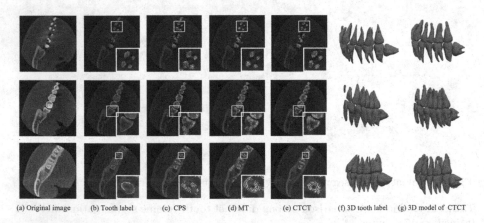

(a) Original image   (b) Tooth label   (c) CPS   (d) MT   (e) CTCT   (f) 3D tooth label   (g) 3D model of CTCT

Fig. 6. Qualitative SSL segmentation results. A closer look reveals clear tooth boundaries at the right bottom corner of each slices.

Table 3. 3D tooth segmentation performance comparison among 4 SSL methods. All models are trained by 9 labelled volumes.

# Unlabeled volume	Method	DSC	IOU	SEN	PPV	HD	ASSD
/	Dense Unet [9]	78.99	65.55	78.81	81.71	4.29	0.57
8	MT [22]	82.66	70.55	83.05	83.11	**2.76**	0.52
	CPS [5]	83.17	71.48	83.10	83.02	4.13	0.55
	DCT [20]	83.10	71.33	83.62	83.10	4.28	0.56
	CTCT [15]	**85.32**	**74.60**	**87.55**	**84.22**	2.81	**0.43**

In Fig. 6, we compare the segmentation details among SSL methods. CPS [5] and MT [22] are not as accurate as CTCT [15] method especially in the tooth root regions. We also compare the 3D tool model based on the segmentation boundaries between ground truth and predicted results of CTCT as shown in sub-figure (f) and (g). It can be seen that the boundary details of CTCT are close to the ground truth.

3.4 Benchmark for Active Learning Based Tooth Volume Segmentation

To reduce the noise effect, we reproduce six AL based medical segmentation methods based on the Attention Unet backbone and present the performances. In Table 4, CEAL [11] achieves the comparable performances as FSL but uses 12% less training data. However, ENT [11] and MAR [13] both have similar performances as the FSL when they are trained on 72 patches. These experiments present that active learning-based tooth volume segmentation is effective but still needs more designs to explore tooth information representation.

Table 4. Evaluation comparison among differnet tooth volume segmentation methods.

# 3D Patches	AL strategy	DSC	IOU	SEN	PPV	HD	ASSD	SO	SD
56	\	81.44	68.86	80.88	83.73	2.71	0.37	92.12	91.85
72	\	85.28	74.41	84.69	86.90	1.88	0.28	94.28	94.20
82	\	**86.60**	**76.45**	86.11	**87.79**	1.72	0.27	95.25	95.20
72	ENT [11]	83.92	72.49	82.44	86.36	1.42	0.27	94.21	94.14
	MAR [13]	84.88	73.86	83.30	87.30	1.63	0.29	94.08	94.03
	CEAL [24]	86.58	76.43	**87.85**	86.01	**1.05**	**0.21**	**95.92**	**95.89**

4   Conclusion

This work is the first to collect and publish a 3D dental dataset CTooth+ with annotated 3D structures of teeth according to quality assessment from experts, and evaluate the tooth volume segmentation on FSL, SSL and AL methods systematically as benchmarks. In future, we will release more data from multiple dental organisations and release more annotations on the tooth structures.

Acknowledgement. The work was supported by the the Natural Science Foundation of China under Grant No. 62002316.

References

1. A,P.: Teeth dataset (2020). https://www.kaggle.com/pushkar34/teeth-dataset
2. Ajaz, A., Kathirvelu, D.: Dental biometrics: computer aided human identification system using the dental panoramic radiographs. In: 2013 International Conference on Communication and Signal Processing, pp. 717–721. IEEE (2013)
3. Alsmadi, M.K.: A hybrid fuzzy c-means and neutrosophic for jaw lesions segmentation. Ain Shams Eng. J. **9**(4), 697–706 (2018)
4. Bui, T.D., Shin, J., Moon, T.: 3D densely convolutional networks for volumetric segmentation. arXiv preprint arXiv:1709.03199 (2017)
5. Chen, X., Yuan, Y., Zeng, G., Wang, J.: Semi-supervised semantic segmentation with cross pseudo supervision. In: Proceedings of the IEEE/CVF Conference on Computer Vision and Pattern Recognition, pp. 2613–2622 (2021)
6. Çiçek, Ö., Abdulkadir, A., Lienkamp, S.S., Brox, T., Ronneberger, O.: 3D U-Net: learning dense volumetric segmentation from sparse annotation. In: Ourselin, S., Joskowicz, L., Sabuncu, M.R., Unal, G., Wells, W. (eds.) MICCAI 2016. LNCS, vol. 9901, pp. 424–432. Springer, Cham (2016). https://doi.org/10.1007/978-3-319-46723-8_49
7. Cui, W., et al.: CTooth: a fully annotated 3d dataset and benchmark for tooth volume segmentation on cone beam computed tomography images, June 2022. arXiv e-prints arXiv:2206.08778
8. Cui, Z., Li, C., Wang, W.: Toothnet: automatic tooth instance segmentation and identification from cone beam CT images. In: Proceedings of the IEEE Conference on Computer Vision and Pattern Recognition, pp. 6368–6377 (2019)
9. Guan, S., Khan, A.A., Sikdar, S., Chitnis, P.V.: Fully dense UNet for 2-d sparse photoacoustic tomography artifact removal. IEEE J. Biomed. Health Inform. **24**(2), 568–576 (2019)
10. He, K., Zhang, X., Ren, S., Sun, J.: Delving deep into rectifiers: surpassing human-level performance on imagenet classification. In: Proceedings of the IEEE International Conference on Computer Vision, pp. 1026–1034 (2015)
11. Hwa, R.: Sample selection for statistical parsing. Comput. Linguist. **30**(3), 253–276 (2004)
12. Isensee, F., et al.: nnU-Net: self-adapting framework for u-net-based medical image segmentation. arXiv preprint arXiv:1809.10486 (2018)
13. Joshi, A.J., Porikli, F., Papanikolopoulos, N.: Multi-class active learning for image classification. In: 2009 IEEE Conference on Computer Vision and Pattern Recognition, pp. 2372–2379. IEEE (2009)
14. Li, Y., et al.: AGMB-transformer: Anatomy-guided multi-branch transformer network for automated evaluation of root canal therapy. IEEE J. Biomed. Health Inform. **26**(4), 1684–1695 (2021)
15. Luo, X., Hu, M., Song, T., Wang, G., Zhang, S.: Semi-supervised medical image segmentation via cross teaching between cnn and transformer. arXiv preprint arXiv:2112.04894 (2021)
16. Lurie, A., Tosoni, G.M., Tsimikas, J., Walker, F., Jr.: Recursive hierarchic segmentation analysis of bone mineral density changes on digital panoramic images. Oral Surg. Oral Med. Oral Pathol. Oral Radiol. **113**(4), 549–558 (2012)
17. Manovich, L.: Inside photoshop. Computational Culture (1) (2011)
18. Milletari, F., Navab, N., Ahmadi, S.A.: V-net: fully convolutional neural networks for volumetric medical image segmentation. In: 2016 Fourth International Conference on 3D Vision (3DV), pp. 565–571. IEEE (2016)

19. Oktay, O., et al.: Attention U-Net: learning where to look for the pancreas. arXiv preprint arXiv:1804.03999 (2018)
20. Qiao, S., Shen, W., Zhang, Z., Wang, B., Yuille, A.: Deep co-training for semi-supervised image recognition. In: Proceedings of the European Conference on Computer Vision (eccv), pp. 135–152 (2018)
21. Silva, G., Oliveira, L., Pithon, M.: Automatic segmenting teeth in x-ray images: trends, a novel data set, benchmarking and future perspectives. Expert Syst. Appl. **107**, 15–31 (2018)
22. Tarvainen, A., Valpola, H.: Mean teachers are better role models: Weight-averaged consistency targets improve semi-supervised deep learning results. Adv. Neural Inf. Process. Syst. **30** (2017)
23. Wang, C.W., et al.: A benchmark for comparison of dental radiography analysis algorithms. Med. Image Anal. **31**, 63–76 (2016)
24. Wang, K., Zhang, D., Li, Y., Zhang, R., Lin, L.: Cost-effective active learning for deep image classification. IEEE Trans. Circuits Syst. Video Technol. **27**(12), 2591–2600 (2016)
25. Yang, S., et al.: A deep learning-based method for tooth segmentation on CBCT images affected by metal artifacts. In: 43rd Annual International Conference of the IEEE Engineering in Medicine and Biology Society (2021)
26. Yu, L., et al.: Automatic 3D cardiovascular MR segmentation with densely-connected volumetric ConvNets. In: Descoteaux, M., Maier-Hein, L., Franz, A., Jannin, P., Collins, D.L., Duchesne, S. (eds.) MICCAI 2017. LNCS, vol. 10434, pp. 287–295. Springer, Cham (2017). https://doi.org/10.1007/978-3-319-66185-8_33
27. Yushkevich, P.A., et al.: User-guided 3d active contour segmentation of anatomical structures: significantly improved efficiency and reliability. Neuroimage **31**(3), 1116–1128 (2006)
28. Zhang, Z., Sabuncu, M.: Generalized cross entropy loss for training deep neural networks with noisy labels. Adv. Neural Inf. Process. Syst. **31** (2018)

Noisy Label Classification Using Label Noise Selection with Test-Time Augmentation Cross-Entropy and NoiseMix Learning

Hansang Lee[1], Haeil Lee[1], Helen Hong[2(✉)], and Junmo Kim[1]

[1] School of Electrical Engineering, Korea Advanced Institute of Science and Technology, Daejeon 34141, Republic of Korea
[2] Department of Software Convergence, Seoul Women's University, Seoul 01797, Republic of Korea
`hlhong@swu.ac.kr`

Abstract. As the size of the dataset used in deep learning tasks increases, the noisy label problem, which is a task of making deep learning robust to the incorrectly labeled data, has become an important task. In this paper, we propose a method of learning noisy label data using the label noise selection with test-time augmentation (TTA) cross-entropy and classifier learning with the NoiseMix method. In the label noise selection, we propose TTA cross-entropy by measuring the cross-entropy to predict the test-time augmented training data. In the classifier learning, we propose the NoiseMix method based on MixUp and BalancedMix methods by mixing the samples from the noisy and the clean label data. In experiments on the ISIC-18 public skin lesion diagnosis dataset, the proposed TTA cross-entropy outperformed the conventional cross-entropy and the TTA uncertainty in detecting label noise data in the label noise selection process. Moreover, the proposed NoiseMix not only outperformed the state-of-the-art methods in the classification performance but also showed the most robustness to the label noise in the classifier learning.

Keywords: Classification · Label noise · Skin lesion diagnosis · Test time augmentation · Mixup

1 Introduction

The noisy label problem represents the task of training a machine learner, mainly a deep neural network, on the training data, which consists of incorrectly labeled data [11]. As the size of the dataset used in deep learning tasks increases, the risk of mislabeled *label noise* data being included in the dataset increases. In addition, when labels are automatically generated from radiological reports to compose large-scale medical image datasets, there is a potential risk for label

© The Author(s), under exclusive license to Springer Nature Switzerland AG 2022
H. V. Nguyen et al. (Eds.): DALI 2022, LNCS 13567, pp. 74–82, 2022.
https://doi.org/10.1007/978-3-031-17027-0_8

noise in medical image datasets [10]. Since the machine learner generally aims to make accurate predictions on all training data, the training data corrupted by the label noise leads to deterioration of the performance of the machine learner. Due to the excellent memorization characteristics of the deep neural networks, the noisy label learning of deep neural networks can be especially challenging.

Several works have been proposed to improve the learning efficiency for noisy label data. Most of them can be divided into two categories, sample-based and model-based methods. The *sample-based* method consists of the *label noise selection* that finds the incorrect label data from the training data, and the *classifier learning* that trains the classifier on the clean label data. Han *et al.* proposed the Co-Teaching method, which selects the label noise data by ranking the cross-entropy loss and trains two networks by teaching each other to improve the robustness [7]. Ju *et al.* suggested the label noise selection with uncertainty estimation and the classifier learning with curriculum learning [10]. The *model-based* method aims to improve the robustness of the network to the noisy labels without the selection of label noise data. Englesson *et al.* proposed that the consistency regularization, e.g., MixUp [16] and AugMix [9] can enhance the robustness of the network to the label noise [5]. Xue *et al.* suggested that self-supervised contrastive learning also can improve the network robustness to the noisy label problems [15].

In this paper, we propose a sample-based method of noisy label learning in medical images to improve both the accuracy of the label noise selection and the robustness of the classifier learning. To achieve this, we propose a test-time augmentation (TTA) cross-entropy for the label noise selection and a NoiseMix method for classifier learning. In the label noise selection, we propose TTA cross-entropy by measuring the cross-entropy to predict the test-time augmented training data. The proposed TTA cross-entropy can avoid the memorization problem of the conventional cross-entropy while improving the label noise detection performance of TTA uncertainty. In the classifier learning, we propose the NoiseMix technique based on MixUp [16] and BalancedMix [6] methods by mixing the samples from the noisy and the clean label data. By modifying the mixing rate of the label noise data in MixUp training, we can further improve the robustness of the classifier to the label noise. We validate the effectiveness of the proposed method on the ISIC-18 public skin lesion diagnosis dataset [1]. In experiments, the proposed TTA cross-entropy outperformed the conventional cross-entropy and the TTA uncertainty in detecting label noise data in the label noise selection process. Moreover, the proposed NoiseMix not only outperformed the state-of-the-art methods in the classification performance but also showed the most robustness to the label noise.

2   Methods

As shown in Fig. 1, our method consists of two main steps. First, we perform label noise selection to separate the clean and the noise label data from the noisy label data using TTA cross-entropy. Second, we perform classifier learning on the noisy training data and the clean label data using the NoiseMix method.

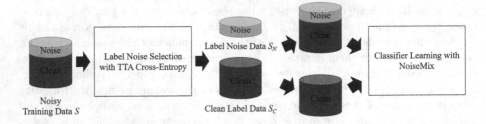

Fig. 1. A pipeline of the proposed method.

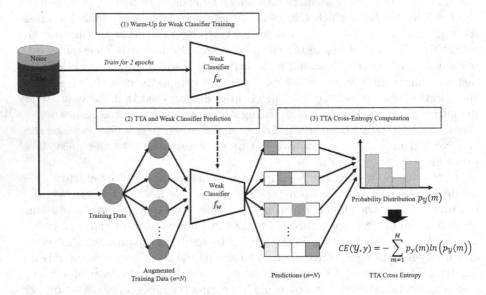

Fig. 2. A pipeline of the proposed label noise selection method.

2.1 Label Noise Selection with Test-Time Augmentation Cross-Entropy

In label noise selection, our aim is to separate the incorrectly-labeled *label noise data* S_N and the correctly-labeled *clean label data* S_C from the entire *noisy label data* $S = \{S_N, S_C\}$. As shown in Fig. 2, our label noise selection method consists of three steps, including (1) warm-up for weak classifier learning, (2) test-time augmentation and weak classifier prediction, and (3) TTA cross-entropy computation.

Warm-Up for Weak Classifier Training. First, we perform *warm-up* that trains the *weak classifier* which will provide the prediction scores of the training data for the label noise selection process. The *weak classifier* $f_w()$ is trained on the entire training data S for a few epochs to prevent the overfitting of the classifier to the incorrect label noise. In experiments, we perform a warm-up on the weak classifier for two epochs.

TTA and Weak Classifier Prediction. Using the trained weak classifier, we compute the prediction scores of the training data to separate the label noise and the clean label data. In the warm-up process, the weak classifier is trained not to prevent the overfitting of the incorrect label noise, but the weak classifier still has a risk of memorizing the label noise data. To avoid the memorization problem of a weak classifier, we perform weak classifier prediction on the augmented training data through affine transformation-based TTA instead of the training data itself.

For a training image-label pair $(x, y) \in S$, we form a set of augmented data $\mathcal{X} = \{x_1, x_2, ..., x_N\}$ with affine transformation $T()$:

$$x_n = T(x, \theta_n) \tag{1}$$

where x_n is the n-th augmented data and θ_n is the n-th parameter setting for affine transformation. We then perform weak classifier prediction on these augmented data to have a set of predicted labels $\mathcal{Y} = \{y_1, y_2, ..., y_N\}$ as follows:

$$y_n = f_w(x_n) \tag{2}$$

where y_n is the n-th predicted label of the augmented training data.

TTA Cross-Entropy Computation. We compute the prediction score using the weak classifier prediction of the augmented training data and select the incorrect label noise data from the training data according to the prediction score. As an efficient prediction score to distinguish the label noise data from the clean label data, we propose a TTA cross-entropy.

For the set of predicted labels of the augmented training data $\mathcal{Y}$ we can form a probability distribution $p_{\mathcal{Y}}$ for unique labels $m = 1, 2, ..., M$ where $p_{\mathcal{Y}}(m)$ is the ratio of the number of y_n with label m among the N predicted labels. For the probability distribution $p_{\mathcal{Y}}$, the conventional *TTA uncertainty* is computed as the entropy of the distribution:

$$H(\mathcal{Y}) = - \sum_{m=1}^{M} p_{\mathcal{Y}}(m) \ln (p_{\mathcal{Y}}(m)). \tag{3}$$

The TTA uncertainty is relatively robust to the memorization problem of the weak classifier compared to the conventional cross-entropy of the training data prediction [10]. However, the TTA uncertainty only evaluates the instability of the label prediction of the augmented data, not whether the training label is correct or incorrect. Thus, it has limitations in missing the cases with incorrect labels but relatively low label uncertainty. To overcome the limitation, we propose a *TTA cross-entropy* to reflect the correctness of training labels to the TTA uncertainty as follows:

$$CE(\mathcal{Y}, y) = - \sum_{m=1}^{M} p_y(m) \ln (p_{\mathcal{Y}}(m)), \tag{4}$$

where p_y is the probability distribution of unique labels for the training label y, where $p_y(m) = 1$ if the training label $y = m$ and $p_y(m) = 0$ if $y \neq m$.

The proposed TTA cross-entropy considers both the label instability of the weak classifier prediction of the augmented training data and the correctness of the training data labels. Thus, the TTA cross-entropy can improve the efficiency of the label noise selection compared to the conventional training data cross-entropy and TTA uncertainty.

2.2 Classifier Training with NoiseMix

We re-train the classifier with the noisy label data and the clean label data obtained from the label noise selection process. We aim to improve the learning efficiency of the clean label data learner with the label noise data while preventing overfitting of the label noise. Inspired by the BalancedMix [6] method for class imbalance learning, we propose the NoiseMix method for noisy label learning by combining two data sampling strategies by means of MixUp [16].

In NoiseMix, we form a mixed training data $(\hat{x}, \hat{y})$ by mixing the clean label data $(x_C, y_C) \in S_C$ with the original training data $(x, y) \in S$ as follows:

$$\hat{x} = \lambda x + (1 - \lambda)x_C, \hat{y} = \lambda y + (1 - \lambda)y_C, \tag{5}$$

where λ is the MixUp coefficient determined as $\lambda \sim \text{Beta}(\alpha, 1)$. The NoiseMix training with $(\hat{x}, \hat{y})$ in 5 not only enables the regularized learning of the clean label data through MixUp but also reflects the effect of re-weighting of the label noise data by mixing them only with the clean label data.

3 Experiments and Results

3.1 Datasets and Experimental Details

The proposed method was validated on the public skin lesion diagnosis dataset of ISIC-18 [1–4, 14][1]. ISIC-18 dataset consists of 10,208 dermoscopic skin lesion images (10,015 for training and 193 for validation) for seven skin disease classes. In this paper, we formulate a binary classification task to classify images of seven skin lesions into benign (8388 for training and 157 for validation) and malignant (1627 for training and 36 for validation,) The benign class includes five skin diseases of AKIEC, BKL, DF, NV, and VASC, whereas the malignant class includes two skin diseases of BCC and MEL.

To construct the noisy label dataset from the ISIC-18 dataset, we generated the *instance-dependent* label noise data [10] instead of random label noise. First, we trained a ResNet-50 on the training data for two epochs with a mini-batch size of 16. Second, using this weak classifier, we measured the cross-entropy loss of the training data. Third, the labels of the $r\%$ of training data with the highest losses were replaced with the labels predicted by the weak classifier, where r is

---

[1] https://challenge2018.isic-archive.com/.

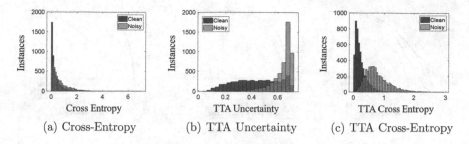

Fig. 3. Histograms of various prediction scores for the label noise (orange) and the clean label (blue) data. (Color figure online)

the ratio of the label noise data. This instance-dependent label noise enables evaluation in a setting similar to a real noisy label environment compared to the random label noise. Here, the ratios of the label noise data to the training data were set to $r = \{10\%, 30\%, 50\%\}$.

In label noise selection of the proposed method, we trained a ResNet-50 for two epochs with a mini-batch size of 16 for weak classifier training. In TTA, a random horizontal flip, a random vertical flip, a random rotation with a degree of $-45° \leq \theta \leq +45°$, a random translation with a shift rate of $(0.1, 0.1)$, and a random scaling with a factor of $1 \leq \sigma \leq 1.2$ were applied. In NoiseMix, the mixing hyper-parameter α determining the MixUp weights $\lambda \sim \text{Beta}(\alpha, 1)$ was set as 0.2.

In experiments, we evaluated (1) the effect of the proposed TTA cross-entropy for the label noise selection and (2) the effect of the proposed NoiseMix for classifier learning. In label noise selection, we compared the proposed TTA cross-entropy with the conventional cross-entropy [5] and the TTA uncertainty [10] by observing the ROC curve and the AUC for detecting the label noise data in the noisy training data. In classifier learning, we compared the accuracy of the proposed NoiseMix with the results of (1) the baseline ResNet-50 [8] trained on the noisy label data S, (2) the DivideMix, a state-of-the-art method for noisy label learning, trained on S, (3) the baseline ResNet-50 trained on the clean label data S_C selected by the proposed TTA cross-entropy, and (4) the baseline MixUp [16] trained on the S_C. Both baseline ResNet-50 trained on S and S_C were trained for 100 epochs with a mini-batch size of 8. In DivideMix, the Inception-ResNet-v2 [13] was trained for 112 epochs with a mini-batch size of 8. In MixUp, the ResNet-18 was trained for 100 epochs with a mini-batch size of 8 and the mixup weight parameter α of 0.2.

3.2 Results

Figure 3 shows the histograms of cross-entropy, TTA uncertainty, and the TTA cross-entropy for the label noise and the clean label data. The prediction score can be considered more valuable as (1) the in-set distribution is concentrated in a limited period and (2) the distributions between two sets are far from each

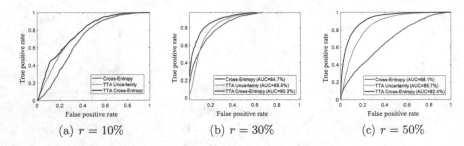

Fig. 4. ROC curves of the cross-entropy (red), TTA uncertainty (blue), and the proposed TTA cross-entropy (black) for detection of the label noise data in the label noise selection process with different label noise ratios r. (Color figure online)

other, so they can be easily separated. In Fig. 3 (a), The cross-entropy of the clean label data is concentrated at the low values, but the cross-entropy of the label noise data is also distributed in the low values, making separation difficult. In Fig. 3 (b), The TTA uncertainty of the label noise data is concentrated at the high values, but the uncertainty of the clean label data is distributed over a wide range of periods, making incorrect detection in label noise selection. In Fig. 3 (c), the distributions of TTA cross-entropy seem to be a mixture of the cross-entropy of clean label data and the TTA uncertainty of the label noise data. Each distribution is distributed in a narrower period, and the overlap between the distributions is smaller than the cross-entropy and the TTA uncertainty. Due to these histogram characteristics, it can be seen that the proposed TTA cross-entropy can be considered a better prediction score for distinguishing the label noise data from the clean label data compared to the cross-entropy and the TTA uncertainty.

Figure 4 shows the ROC curves and AUCs of proposed and comparative label noise selection methods for detecting the label noise data. It can be observed that the label noise selection with cross-entropy shows low detection performance

Table 1. Performance comparison for various methods and label noise ratios r.

Methods	Label noise ratios		
	10%	30%	50%
ResNet-50 [8]	85.8	80.9	66.8
DivideMix [12]	81.4	79.8	73.6
TTA Cross-Entropy + ResNet-50	81.4	81.4	80.8
TTA Cross-Entropy + MixUp	85.4	82.5	75.1
TTA Cross-Entropy + NoiseMix (Ours)	**86.7**	**83.8**	**85.5**

in separating label noise and clean label data. This is because the network can be easily overfitted on the medical images due to similar appearance, and the cross-entropy is vulnerable to the memorization problem of the overfitted weak classifier. The memorization problem seems mostly avoided by applying TTA uncertainty, and the proposed TTA cross-entropy further improves the detection performance of the label noise data regardless of label noise ratios r.

Table 1 shows the accuracies of the proposed and the comparative methods in classifier learning for different label noise ratios r. The performance of noisy label learning can be evaluated from two perspectives: (1) For each label noise ratio, the method with the highest accuracy can be considered as the *best* noisy label learner. (2) For the increase in the label noise ratio, the method with the smallest decrease in performance can be considered as the *most robust* noisy label learner. From the highest accuracy perspective, it can be observed that the proposed method with NoiseMix outperformed not only the baseline ResNet-50 and MixUp but also the state-of-the-art DivideMix regardless of label noise ratios. In the noise robustness perspective, when the label noise ratio r increases from 10% to 50%, the MixUp and DivideMix decrease by 10.3%p and 7.8%p, respectively, while the performance of the proposed method decreases only 1.2%p. It can be confirmed that the proposed NoiseMix enables not only the best performance but also the most robust noisy label learning.

4   Conclusions

In this paper, we proposed a method of learning noisy label data using the label noise selection with TTA cross-entropy and the classifier learning with the NoiseMix method. In the label noise selection, the proposed TTA cross-entropy improved the accuracy of selecting label noise data by preventing the memorization problem of the conventional cross-entropy and reflecting the label correctness to the TTA uncertainty. In the classifier learning, the proposed NoiseMix enhanced the robustness by reflecting the effect of re-weighting the label noise data to the conventional MixUp. As a result, our TTA cross-entropy outperformed the conventional cross-entropy and TTA uncertainty in noisy label noise selection. Furthermore, our NoiseMix outperformed the existing training techniques without designing loss functions or weighting schemes.

Acknowledgments. This work was supported by the National Research Foundation of Korea(NRF) grant funded by the Korea government(MSIT) (No. 2020 R1A2C1102140), and the Korea Medical Device Development Fund grant funded by the Korea government (the Ministry of Science and ICT, the Ministry of Trade, Industry and Energy, the Ministry of Health & Welfare, the Ministry of Food and Drug Safety) (Project Number: 9991007550, KMDF_PR_20200901_0269).

References

1. Codella, N.C.F., et al.: Skin lesion analysis toward melanoma detection: a challenge at the 2017 international symposium on biomedical imaging (ISBI), hosted by the international skin imaging collaboration (ISIC). In: 2018 IEEE 15th International Symposium on Biomedical Imaging (ISBI 2018), pp. 168–172 (2018)
2. Codella, N.C.F., et al.: Skin lesion analysis toward melanoma detection: a challenge at the 2017 international symposium on biomedical imaging (ISBI), hosted by the international skin imaging collaboration (ISIC). CoRR arXiv:abs/1710.05006 (2017)
3. Codella, N.C.F., et al.: Skin lesion analysis toward melanoma detection 2018: a challenge hosted by the international skin imaging collaboration (ISIC). CoRR arXiv:abs/1902.03368 (2019)
4. Combalia, M., et al.: Bcn20000: dermoscopic lesions in the wild (2019)
5. Englesson, E., Azizpour, H.: Consistency regularization can improve robustness to label noise. CoRR arXiv:abs/2110.01242 (2021)
6. Galdran, A., Carneiro, G., González Ballester, M.A.: Balanced-mixup for highly imbalanced medical image classification. In: De Bruijne, M., et al. (eds.) MICCAI 2021. LNCS, vol. 12905, pp. 323–333. Springer, Cham (2021). https://doi.org/10.1007/978-3-030-87240-3_31
7. Han, B., et al.: Co-teaching: robust training of deep neural networks with extremely noisy labels. In: Bengio, S., Wallach, H., Larochelle, H., Grauman, K., Cesa-Bianchi, N., Garnett, R. (eds.) Advances in Neural Information Processing Systems, vol. 31. Curran Associates, Inc. (2018)
8. He, K., Zhang, X., Ren, S., Sun, J.: Deep residual learning for image recognition. In: Proceedings of the IEEE Conference on Computer Vision and Pattern Recognition (CVPR), June 2016
9. Hendrycks, D., Mu, N., Cubuk, E.D., Zoph, B., Gilmer, J., Lakshminarayanan, B.: AugMix: a simple data processing method to improve robustness and uncertainty. In: Proceedings of the International Conference on Learning Representations (ICLR) (2020)
10. Ju, L., et al.: Improving medical images classification with label noise using dual-uncertainty estimation. IEEE Trans. Med. Imaging **41**(6), 1533–1546 (2022)
11. Karimi, D., Dou, H., Warfield, S.K., Gholipour, A.: Deep learning with noisy labels: exploring techniques and remedies in medical image analysis. Med. Image Anal. **65**, 101759 (2020)
12. Li, J., Socher, R., Hoi, S.C.: Dividemix: learning with noisy labels as semi-supervised learning. In: International Conference on Learning Representations (2020)
13. Szegedy, C., Ioffe, S., Vanhoucke, V., Alemi, A.A.: Inception-v4, inception-resnet and the impact of residual connections on learning. In: Proceedings of the Thirty-First AAAI Conference on Artificial Intelligence, pp. 4278–4284 (2017)
14. Tschandl, P., Rosendahl, C., Kittler, H.: The ham10000 dataset, a large collection of multi-source dermatoscopic images of common pigmented skin lesions. Sci. Data **5**(1), 180161 (2018)
15. Xue, Y., Whitecross, K., Mirzasoleiman, B.: Investigating why contrastive learning benefits robustness against label noise. CoRR arXiv:abs/2201.12498 (2022)
16. Zhang, H., Cisse, M., Dauphin, Y.N., Lopez-Paz, D.: Mixup: beyond empirical risk minimization. In: International Conference on Learning Representations (2018)

CSGAN: Synthesis-Aided Brain MRI Segmentation on 6-Month Infants

Xin Tang[1], Jiadong Zhang[1], Yongsheng Pan[1], Yuyao Zhang[1], and Feng Shi[2(✉)]

[1] School of Biomedical Engineering, ShanghaiTech University,
Shanghai 201210, China
[2] Shanghai United Imaging Intelligence Co., Ltd., Shanghai 200230, China
feng.shi@uii-ai.com

Abstract. Due to the early myelination process in infant brain development, white matter (WM) tissue demonstrates isointense with gray matter (GM) tissue in brain MRI for infants around 6 months. This process
results in extremely low brain tissue intensity contrast between WM and
GM in MRI, thus leading to a great challenge for experts to manually
delineate brain tissue boundaries. Hence, for brain tissue segmentation
task of 6-month-old infant MRI, the number of training data with reliable
labels is quite limited. Inspired by the recent progress in the image synthesis field, we propose to use the largely available 12-month brain MR data
and their relatively reliable segmentation masks to synthesize 6-month-
like brain MR data with corresponding segmentation masks. Briefly, we
design a novel model called CSGAN for 6-month MR image synthesis.
CSGAN introduces a spatially-adaptive normalization (SPADE) module
in the generators of CycleGAN, by embedding semantic information into
networks to keep the brain anatomical structure consistent across 6-month
and 12-month brain MRI. After that, we train an initial segmentation
model on these augmented data to overcome the isointense problem in
6-months infant MRI. In experiments, the segmentation model is further
fine-tuned on the real 6-month MR images from the public dataset iSeg-
2019, and the evaluation results demonstrate superior performance of our
method compared to state-of-the-art studies.

Keywords: Infant brain segmentation · MR image synthesis · Data
augmentation

1 Introduction

The neonatal brain develops at a rapid rate throughout the first year. It doubles
in brain tissue size at this stage, along with developing a wide range of cognitive and motor functions. This early period is critical for the diagnosis of many
neurodevelopmental and neuropsychiatric disorders, such as schizophrenia and
autism. For example, Shen et al. reported that high-risk infants, who later developed Autism spectrum disorder (ASD), had increased extra-axial cerebrospinal
fluid (EA-CSF) volume in 6–24 months [8]. Thus, it is crucial to generate an

H. V. Nguyen et al. (Eds.): DALI 2022, LNCS 13567, pp. 83–91, 2022.
https://doi.org/10.1007/978-3-031-17027-0_9

accurate segmentation of MRI into different regions of interest, for example, white matter (WM), gray matter (GM), and cerebrospinal fluid (CSF) [9], for further identifying biomarkers and study both normal and abnormal early brain development.

However, compared with MR images acquired at the early adult-like phase (i.e., greater 9-month-old), the contrast in those acquired at the isointense phase (around 6-month-old) is extremely low, thus leading to ambiguous boundaries between different tissues. As shown in Fig. 1, in the adult-like phase, we can easily identify different brain tissues (such as WM, GM, and CSF) by their intensity distributions. By contrast, the large overlapping of tissue intensity distribution at the isointense phase makes it hard to delineate neonatal brain tissues. Thus, how to achieve robust and accurate segmentation results from MRI at the isointense phase is still an open challenge.

In recent years, deep neural networks (DNNs) show great potential in medical image segmentation tasks, and are well exploited for adult brain tissue segmentation. Unfortunately, the limited number of reliable labeled MR data at the isointense phase greatly weakens DNNs' advantages in this segmentation task. Though some works proposed to use task-specific networks [2,11] or ensemble and other strategies [3,4] on this task, the improvement is still limited, and sometimes involves over-fitting problems.

Considering that there are sufficient MR data in the adult-like phase, which can be precisely segmented by physicians and used as ground-truth (GT) labels, we thus intend to use these 12-month MR data with reliable GT to guide 6-month MR data segmentation. Specifically, we generate 6-month-like MR data from corresponding 12-month MR data with image synthesis methods. It's worth mentioning that for each 12-month MRI, we only transfer its tissue appearance style so that it looks like 6-month MRI. In this way, the tissue segmentation in 12-month MRI can be propagated to the synthesized 6-month image.

Then we use these augmented large amounts of 6-month-like MR data to train the segmentation network, which learns how to achieve correct segmentation results with these 6-month style distributions. Then, the well-trained segmentation network can be transferred to real 6-month data via a fine-tuning process to further boost its performance.

Based on this idea, the problem to be solved becomes how to generate qualified 6-month-like MR data from corresponding 12-month MR data. Considering that paired 6-month and 12-month MR data are hard to obtain and CycleGAN's good performance on unpaired data, we choose it as our basic model to achieve the synthesis task. In order to keep the brain's anatomical structure consistent across two phases, we also involve spatially-adaptive normalization (SPADE) in the generators of CycleGAN by embedding semantic information into networks. We evaluate our methods on iSeg-2019 datasets, and the results demonstrate superior performance.

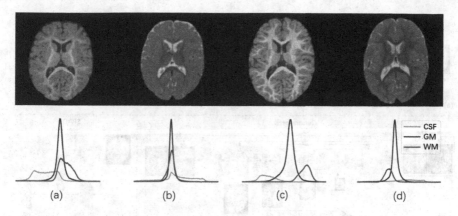

Fig. 1. Representative longitudinal MR images and corresponding tissue intensity distributions from the same individual. (a) T1 image at 6-month; (b) T2 image at 6-month; (c) T1 image at 12-month; (d) T2 image at 12-month. Note that the brain size in 12-month is slightly larger than that of 6-month, and we roughly select a similar slice to show the anatomy after affine alignment.

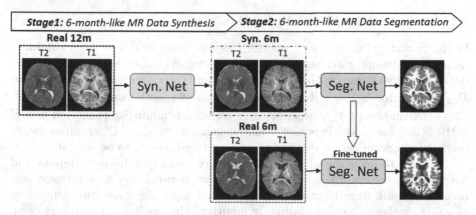

Fig. 2. Overview of proposed synthesis-guided 6-month MR data segmentation method.

2   Method

As mentioned above, our methods have two stages (See Fig. 2). The first stage aims to generate qualified 6-month-like MR data from 12-month MR data, and the second stage is to use augmented 6-month data to train a segmentation model and transfer it to real 6-month MR data.

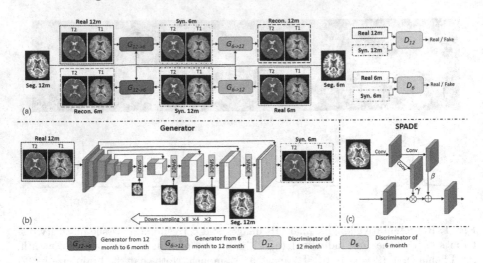

Fig. 3. Architecture of proposed CSGAN for 6-month-like MR data synthesis.

2.1 6-Month-Like MR Data Synthesis

In the first stage, we choose CycleGAN as our basic model to learn the high-dimensional mapping across two different phases. As illustrated in Fig. 3(a), we define two generators (i.e. $G_{12\to6}$ and $G_{6\to12}$) and two discriminators (i.e. D_6 and D_{12}). Generator $G_{12\to6}$ is designed to synthesize 6-month samples $\{y_i\}_{i=1}^{N}$ from 12-month samples $\{x_i\}_{i=1}^{N}$, where $x_i \in X$ is the early adult-like phase and $y_i \in Y$ is the isointense phase. It is vice versa for generator $G_{6\to12}$. Discriminators are designed to encourage synthesized images and real images to be similar.

In order to keep the anatomical structure consistent between inputs and outputs, we also involve another segmentation network S_{12} to get tissue segmentation mask from 12-month MR data, and input the mask into generators to guide synthesis. Instead of directly inputting the mask into generators as an additional channel, we find a more efficient way to embed the semantic information in the synthesis process by taking good advantage of SPADE [6]. The generator and SPADE module are illustrated in Fig. 3(b) and 3(c). The generator takes U-net as a basic model, and we add SPADE module in each layer of decoder. The discriminator architecture is the same as PatchGAN in [12]. As for the SPADE block, we use both feature maps and 12-month segmentation masks, which is down-sampled to match feature maps' size in a different layer, as inputs. Specifically, we can get modulation parameters $\gamma \in \mathbb{R}^{1\times C\times H\times W}$ and $\beta \in \mathbb{R}^{1\times C\times H\times W}$ from down-sampled segmentation mask $m \in \mathbb{R}^{B\times3\times H\times W}$ in each layer through simple conv-layers, where B denotes the sample number in the current mini-batch, and C, H, W denotes channel, height and width of feature maps respectively. These two parameters can normalize feature maps $f \in \mathbb{R}^{B\times C\times H\times W}$ according to learned semantic information. The SPADE is formulated as:

$$\gamma_{c,h,w}(m)\frac{f_{b,c,h,w} - \mu_c}{\sigma_c} + \beta_{c,h,w}(m). \tag{1}$$

where $b \in B, c \in C, h \in H, w \in W$ are the pixel location of feature maps and μ_c and σ_c are the mean and standard deviation of the feature maps in channel c. μ_c and σ_c can be calculated as follow:

$$\mu_c = \frac{1}{BHW} \sum_{b,h,w} f_{b,c,h,w}. \tag{2}$$

$$\sigma_c = \sqrt{\frac{1}{NHW} \sum_{b,h,w} \left((f_{b,c,h,w})^2 - (\mu_c)^2 \right)}. \tag{3}$$

In the synthesis stage, we get 12-month segmentation masks with the existing algorithm [9], and combine them with a small set of 6-month images with ground-truth segmentation masks to jointly train the CSGAN. While alternatively training generators (i.e. $G_{12 \to 6}$ and $G_{12 \to 6}$) and discriminators (i.e. D_6 and D_{12}). The loss function of CSGAN is defined as follows:

$$
\begin{aligned}
\mathcal{L}_{\mathrm{CSGAN}}(G_{12 \to 6}, G_{6 \to 12}, D_{12}, D_6) = &\ \mathcal{L}_{GAN}(G_{12 \to 6}, D_6) \\
&+ \mathcal{L}_{GAN}(G_{6 \to 12}, D_{12}) \\
&+ \lambda \mathcal{L}_{\mathrm{cycle}}(G_{12 \to 6}, G_{6 \to 12}) \\
&+ \xi \mathcal{L}_{\mathrm{identity}}(G_{12 \to 6}, G_{6 \to 12}).
\end{aligned}
\tag{4}
$$

As shown in Eq. (4), the loss function has four terms. The first term and second term are adversarial loss [5] for two generators and corresponding discriminators, which is defined as follow:

$$
\begin{aligned}
\mathcal{L}_{\mathrm{GAN}}(G_{12 \to 6}, D_6) = &\ \mathbb{E}_{y \sim p_{\mathrm{data}}(y)}[\log D_6(y)] \\
&+ \mathbb{E}_{x \sim p_{\mathrm{data}}(x)}[\log(1 - D_6(G_{12 \to 6}(x)))]
\end{aligned}
\tag{5}
$$

$$
\begin{aligned}
\mathcal{L}_{\mathrm{GAN}}(G_{6 \to 12}, D_{12}) = &\ \mathbb{E}_{x \sim p_{\mathrm{data}}(x)}[\log D_{12}(x)] \\
&+ \mathbb{E}_{y \sim p_{\mathrm{data}}(y)}[\log(1 - D_{12}(G_{6 \to 12}(y)))]
\end{aligned}
\tag{6}
$$

The third term $\mathcal{L}_{\mathrm{cycle}}$ is cycle consistency loss, which is defined as follows

$$
\begin{aligned}
\mathcal{L}_{\mathrm{cyc}}(G_{12 \to 6}, G_{6 \to 12}) = &\ \mathbb{E}_{x \sim X}[\|G_{6 \to 12}(G_{12 \to 6}(x)) - x\|_1] \\
&+ \mathbb{E}_{y \sim Y}[\|G_{12 \to 6}(G_{6 \to 12}(y)) - y\|_1],
\end{aligned}
\tag{7}
$$

and the fourth term, identity loss $\mathcal{L}_{identity}$, is introduced to constrain the feature recognition of the generator.

$$
\begin{aligned}
\mathcal{L}_{\mathrm{identity}}(G_{12 \to 6}, G_{6 \to 12}) = &\ \mathbb{E}_{x \sim X}[\|G_{6 \to 12}(x) - x\|_1] \\
&+ \mathbb{E}_{y \sim Y}[\|G_{12 \to 6}(y) - y\|_1].
\end{aligned}
\tag{8}
$$

In Eqs. (4), λ and ξ are two hyper-parameters to balance the importance of the four terms.

2.2 6-month-like MR Data Segmentation

In this second stage, we use the generated 6-month-like MR data with accurate tissue segmentation masks to train a robust segmentation network. This large amount of augmented 6-month-like data can help the segmentation network learn how to get correct segmentation results with 6-month style distribution. With this well-trained segmentation network, we fine-tune it on real 6-month MR data to build the final robust 6-month brain segmentation network. In this stage, we adopt U-net as our segmentation model [7] by considering its great performance on medical image segmentation tasks. We use both cross-entropy loss and dice loss as segmentation loss functions to supervise model training.

3   Experiments and Results

3.1 Datasets

We use the public NDAR dataset[1] and iSeg 2019 dataset[2] [10]. For NDAR dataset, there are 127 cases of longitudinal data with 6-month and 12-month infant brain MR images. Every case has both T1 and T2 weighted MR images with well-labeled tissue segmentation masks on 12-month data. The resolution of MR data is $256 \times 256 \times 150$ with a voxel size of $1.0 \times 1.0 \times 1.0\,mm^3$. As for iSeg 2019 dataset, there are only 10 cases of 6-month infant brain MR data available. Every case has both T1 and T2 weighted MR images with well-labeled tissue segmentation masks on 6-month data. The resolution of MR data is $144 \times 192 \times 256$ with a voxel size of $1.0 \times 1.0 \times 1.0\,\mathrm{mm}^3$.

Considering the size variation across two different phases, we want to use registration algorithms to make their size similar. Specifically, we use ANTS algorithm [1] to align 12-month MR data with 6-month data with affine and nonlinear transformations.

Before inputting images into the network, we normalize the intensity value into a range of [0, 1] by min-max normalization. 87 subjects of NDAR datasets are used to train our CSGAN network and the rest 40 subjects of NDAR dataset are used for validation. Then we train the segmentation network with these 40 synthesized 6-month-like data and fine-tune it with 8 subjects from iSeg-2019 dataset in each five-fold cross-validation. The rest 2 subjects from iSeg-2019 dataset are used to evaluate segmentation performance.

3.2 Implement Details

In the first stage, the initial learning rate is set as 0.0002 and decays 1% every epoch after 100 epochs (total 250 epochs). The hyper-parameters λ and ξ in Eq. (4) are set as 10 and 0.5 respectively. In the second stage, the initial learning rate is set as 0.0001 and decays 1% every epoch after 100 epochs (total 200 epochs).

---

[1] https://www.nitrc.org/.
[2] https://iseg2019.web.unc.edu/.

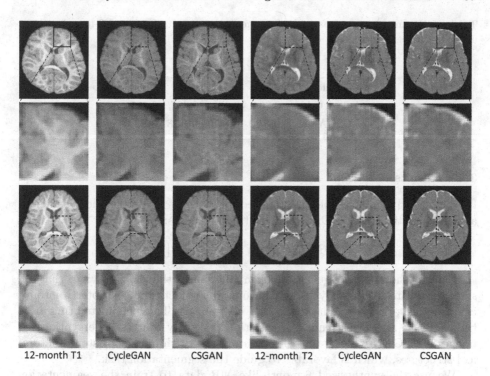

Fig. 4. Image synthesis results for CycleGAN and the proposed CSGAN. Left panel shows the T1 image results and the right panel shows the T2 image results. The top 2 rows demonstrate the gray/white matter tissue contrast changes, and the bottom 2 rows show possible mode collapse in CycleGAN while successfully retrieved in CSGAN.

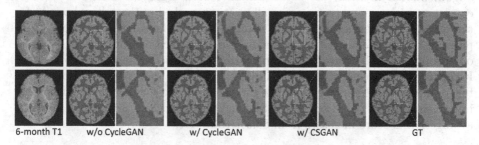

Fig. 5. Visual comparison of real 6-month MR data segmentation results.

All experiments are conducted on PyTorch platform with one NVIDIA TITAN RTX 2080Ti GPU (12GB). We choose ADAM optimizer to optimize networks in two stages.

Table 1. Quantitative comparison of segmentation results from real 6-month images using U-net segmentation model.

Method	CSF	GM	WM	Avg
w/o CycleGAN	0.851	0.832	0.829	0.836
w/ CycleGAN	0.864	0.859	0.837	0.855
w/ CSGAN	**0.890**	**0.866**	**0.858**	**0.871**

3.3 Results

For quantitative analysis of our proposed method, we adapt the dice coefficient as the evaluation metric. Dice coefficient is defined as:

$$DICE = 2 A \cap B|/(|A| + |B|) \tag{9}$$

Figure 4 shows images generated from different methods. It's obvious that the synthesized images from CycleGAN have more artifacts and corrupted anatomical structures, which are marked in the yellow boxes. These artifacts bring more the challenge for downstream segmentation tasks. By contrast, the synthesized images of CSGAN is closer to real 6-month image with more consistent anatomical structures, which is favorable to guide the segmentation task.

We use the synthesized 6-month-like MR data to train the segmentation model and fine-tune it on real 6-month MR data and get pretty good segmentation performance. The visualization results of the two cases are shown in Fig. 5. Compare with non-augmentation method (i.e. w/o CycleGAN) and CycleGAN-augumentation method, the segmentation results from our method are more consistent with ground truth, especially tissues marked in the yellow box. As for the quantitative results in Table 1, we also can get the same conclusion. Compared with non-augmentation methods, the DICE scores from CycleGAN and our proposed CSGAN are higher, indicating better segmentation performance. It proves the proposed synthesis-guided 6-month MR data segmentation is useful to improve performance. And our further proposed CSGAN model has more improvement, the DICE score of CSF increases from 85.1% to 89.0% and the average DICE score increases from 85.5% to 87.1%.

4   Conclusion

In this paper, we proposed to use large amount 12-month brain MR data with reliable segmentation masks to guide 6-month brain MR data segmentation. In order to keep anatomical structure consistent across different phases, we further proposed CSGAN. Specifically, we adopt segmentation masks as additional inputs and use SPADE to embed semantic information. We use public data to evaluate the proposed method, and the experiments show great improvement in our method with better segmentation accuracy on 6-month MR data.

References

1. Avants, B.B., Tustison, N.J., Song, G., Cook, P.A., Klein, A., Gee, J.C.: A reproducible evaluation of ants similarity metric performance in brain image registration. Neuroimage **54**(3), 2033–2044 (2011)
2. Bui, T.D., Shin, J., Moon, T.: 3d densely convolutional networks for volumetric segmentation. arXiv preprint arXiv:1709.03199 (2017)
3. Dolz, J., Desrosiers, C., Wang, L., Yuan, J., Shen, D., Ayed, I.B.: Deep cnn ensembles and suggestive annotations for infant brain mri segmentation. Comput. Med. Imaging Graph. **79**, 101660 (2020)
4. Gandhi, R., Hong, Y.: Mda-net: Multi-dimensional attention-based neural network for 3d image segmentation. In: 2021 IEEE 18th International Symposium on Biomedical Imaging (ISBI), pp. 822–826. IEEE (2021)
5. Goodfellow, I., et al.: Generative adversarial nets. In: Advances in Neural Information Processing Systems, vol. 27 (2014)
6. Park, T., Liu, M.Y., Wang, T.C., Zhu, J.Y.: Semantic image synthesis with spatially-adaptive normalization. In: Proceedings of the IEEE/CVF Conference on Computer Vision and Pattern Recognition, pp. 2337–2346 (2019)
7. Ronneberger, Olaf, Fischer, Philipp, Brox, Thomas: U-Net: convolutional networks for biomedical image segmentation. In: Navab, Nassir, Hornegger, Joachim, Wells, William M.., Frangi, Alejandro F.. (eds.) MICCAI 2015. LNCS, vol. 9351, pp. 234–241. Springer, Cham (2015). https://doi.org/10.1007/978-3-319-24574-4_28
8. Shen, M.D., et al.: Increased extra-axial cerebrospinal fluid in high-risk infants who later develop autism. Biol. Psychiat. **82**(3), 186–193 (2017)
9. Shi, F., Fan, Y., Tang, S., Gilmore, J.H., Lin, W., Shen, D.: Neonatal brain image segmentation in longitudinal mri studies. Neuroimage **49**(1), 391–400 (2010)
10. Sun, Y., et al.: Multi-site infant brain segmentation algorithms: the iseg-2019 challenge. IEEE Trans. Med. Imaging **40**(5), 1363–1376 (2021)
11. Wang, L., et al.: Benchmark on automatic six-month-old infant brain segmentation algorithms: the iseg-2017 challenge. IEEE Trans. Med. Imaging **38**(9), 2219–2230 (2019)
12. Zhu, J.Y., Park, T., Isola, P., Efros, A.A.: Unpaired image-to-image translation using cycle-consistent adversarial networks. In: Proceedings of the IEEE International Conference on Computer Vision, pp. 2223–2232 (2017)

A Stratified Cascaded Approach for Brain Tumor Segmentation with the Aid of Multi-modal Synthetic Data

Yasmina Al Khalil[1]([✉]), Aymen Ayaz[1], Cristian Lorenz[2], Jürgen Weese[2], Josien Pluim[1], and Marcel Breeuwer[1,3]

[1] Eindhoven University of Technology, Eindhoven, The Netherlands
{y.al.khalil,a.ayaz,j.pluim,m.breeuwer}@tue.nl
[2] Philips Research Laboratories, Hamburg, Germany
{cristian.lorenz,juergen.weese}@philips.com
[3] Philips Healthcare, MR R&D - Clinical Science, Best, The Netherlands

Abstract. Gliomas are one of the most widespread and aggressive forms of brain tumors. Accurate brain tumor segmentation is crucial for evaluation, monitoring and treatment of gliomas. Recent advances in deep learning methods have made a significant step towards a robust and automated brain tumor segmentation. However, due to the variation in shape and location of gliomas, as well as their appearance across different tumor grades, obtaining an accurate and generalizable segmentation model is still a challenge. To alleviate this, we propose a cascaded segmentation pipeline, aimed at introducing more robustness to segmentation performance through data stratification. In other words, we train separate models per tumor grade, aided with synthetic brain tumor images generated through conditional generative adversarial networks. To handle the variety in size, shape and location of tumors, we utilize a localization module, focusing the training and inference in the vicinity of the tumor. Finally, to identify which tumor grade segmentation model to utilize at inference time, we train a dense, attention-based 3D classification model. The obtained results suggest that both stratification and the addition of synthetic data to training significantly improve the segmentation performance, whereby up to 55% of test cases exhibit a performance improvement by more than 5% and up to 40% of test cases exhibit an improvement by more than 10% in Dice score.

Keywords: Brain tumor segmentation · Synthesis · Data stratification

1 Introduction

Accurate and consistent brain tumor segmentation is crucial for diagnosis, treatment planning and post-treatment assessment of cancer patients. Gliomas are

Supplementary Information The online version contains supplementary material available at https://doi.org/10.1007/978-3-031-17027-0_10.

the most common type of brain tumors that are typically grouped into low-grade, usually mild, gliomas (LGGs) and high-grade gliomas (HGGs), typically malignant and more aggressive [3]. Brain tumor evaluation and diagnosis is mainly derived from magnetic resonance imaging (MRI) scans, with segmentation being the preliminary step. The current gold standard in brain tumor segmentation is manual tracing by professional radiologists, which is a tedious process prone to inter-rater variability. Thus, automatic or semi-automatic segmentation approaches have been a topic of interest in the last decade. Recently, convolutional neural networks (CNNs) have gained popularity [1,6,10] by exhibiting promising results for brain tumor segmentation, particularly on benchmark datasets, such as the Multi-modal Brain Tumor Segmentation (BraTS) challenge [8].

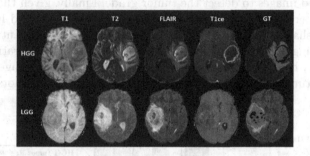

Fig. 1. Differences in appearance between LGG and HGG tumors across four different MRI contrasts. Typical tumor sub-regions of interest are depicted in the last column, consisting of edema, enhancing tumor and non-advancing/necrotic tumor. (Color figure online)

Typical deep learning approaches targeting brain tumor segmentation are usually trained ad hoc on all available data, omitting additional information about the patient genetic characteristics or tumor grade. However, recent studies suggest a strong potential towards improving such methods by taking into account this latent information [11]. In fact, the appearance of gliomas significantly varies between LGG and HGG and across different imaging modalities (see Fig. 1). We hypothesize that deep learning methods for brain tumor segmentation can be significantly improved by distributing model training and application per tumor grade. However, this approach significantly reduces the amount of data available for training, which is further exacerbated by imbalance with respect to the tumor grade type. To address this, we propose a cascaded segmentation approach, used to localize and classify the tumor area and perform a fine-grained tumor region segmentation per tumor grade. The training of pipeline components is aided with synthesized brain tumor images, obtained from conditional generative adversarial networks (GANs) trained per tumor grade.

2   Methods

We propose a segmentation pipeline aimed at addressing the particular challenges of brain tumor segmentation, depicted in Fig. 2. First, to address the problem of varying tumor tissue proportion and size in brain MR images, we utilize a tumor detection network, aimed at identifying the region of interest in the vicinity of tumorous tissue. Once the whole tumor is roughly segmented, all multi-modal MR images used for training are cropped and utilized for training an additional module for fine-grained tumor region segmentation. To address the differences between tumor grades, we propose a stratified segmentation approach and introduce two separate segmentation models trained on LGG and HGG images. Since this approach requires prior knowledge of tumor grade, which is typically not provided at inference time, we add a classification module trained on the cropped images to detect the tumor grade. Finally, given the unbalanced dataset (smaller amount of LGG images compared to HGG) and high variability in tumor shapes, sizes and appearance, we propose to augment the training data by utilizing a multi-modal conditional synthesis using generative adversarial networks, where we generate multi-contrast brain tumor images containing variations in tumor shape and sizes of both LGG and HGG tumors.

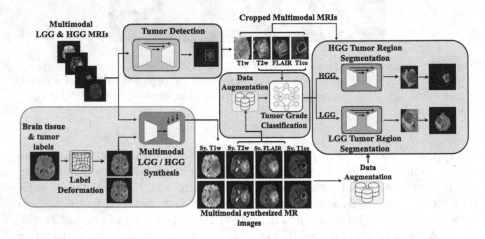

Fig. 2. An overview of the stratified brain tumor segmentation and synthesis pipeline.

2.1   Stratified Conditional GANs for Brain Tumor Image Synthesis

GANs conditioned on auxiliary data of brain tissue and tumor class labels are used for tumor image synthesis. BRATS T1w brain tumor MRI data (of both HGG and LGG grade) is applied to the brain classification tool, based on the fully convolutional multi-scale network architecture [4]. The white matter, gray matter and CSF labels generated covering the full brain are combined with the available manual annotations of edema, enhancing tumor and non-advancing/necrotic tumor. The multi-modal structural data along with the combined six class labels is used for training the multi-modal image synthesis networks, per tumor grade. No data augmentation strategies are used and 2D center cropping and noise-only slice cropping in transverse direction is performed as a pre-processing step. An overview of the synthesis approach is depicted in Fig. 3. 2D conditional SPatially-Adaptive (DE)normalization (SPADE) GAN model [9] is used for multi-modal brain synthesis.

The network is trained using the Adam optimizer with a learning rate of 0.0002, batch size of 12 on three NVIDIA TITAN Xp GPUs. The remaining training parameters, architecture and losses are defined as in [9]. Four separate 2D SPADE GANs are trained while slicing across axial direction for T1w, T2w, T1ce and FLAIR brain tumor MRI respectively, for both LGG and HGG tumor grades. The synthesis is performed on complete full brain label maps to provide more guidance during image generation, leading to realistic appearing brain tumor images. At inference, multi-slice 2D brain multi-modal MRI volumes are synthesized for a set of LGG and HGG tumor labels that are not seen by the networks during training. To include more variability in tumor shapes and sizes, the unseen tumor labels are deformed using elastic transform, dilation and erosion. Please refer to Appendix A of the Supplementary material for a detailed description of the whole synthesis pipeline.

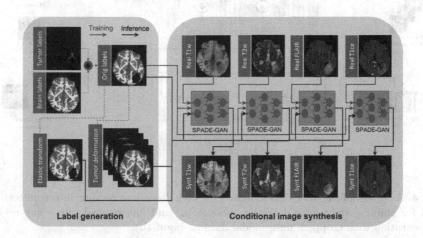

Fig. 3. An overview of the conditional synthesis approach used for variable multi-modal brain tumor MR image synthesis. Six class labels generated covering full brain and tumor along multi-modal MR tumor data are used to train multi-modal conditional image synthesis networks. The multi-modal inference is made on unseen, elastic transformed and tumor-deformed (dilated and eroded) set of labels.

2.2   Whole Tumor Detection

Brain tumor lesions affect a very small portion of the brain, which impedes the training of segmentation models. To alleviate this, we first detect the tumorous tissue in the provided multi-modal MR images, by utilizing a variant of a standard 3D U-Net with added residual and dense interconnections between layers [7,12], depicted in Fig. 4. The network is trained on all four modalities, using both LGG and HGG images, where all brain voxels have previously been normalized to an intensity range from [0,1], followed by 98th percentile contrast stretching. The input patch size is set to $128 \times 128 \times 128$, with a batch size of 5. We used Adam for optimization, with an initial learning rate of 5×10^{-4} and a weight decay of $5 \times e^{-5}$. The loss function used is the modified Dice coefficient, adapted for binary segmentation tasks with imbalanced data. The training is conducted on two NVIDIA TITAN Xp GPUs for a maximum of 500 epochs with a polynomial learning rate decay [5]. Data augmentation is applied on the fly during training. We apply connected component analysis on the obtained binary output to remove any false positive predictions, followed by cropping the multi-modal images around the tumor. The proposed approach achieves a Dice score of 0.921 on a test set containing both HGG and LGG tumors.

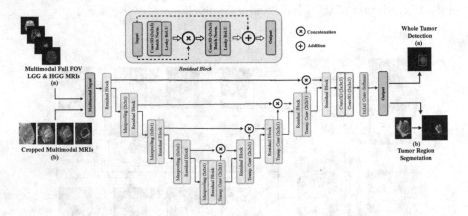

Fig. 4. A variant of the 3D U-Net architecture with dense and residual interconnections used for training the tumor detection module (a) and fine-grained tumor sub-region segmentation with cropped multi-modal data as input (b).

2.3   Brain Tumor Grade Classification

We utilize a 3D densely connected convolutional neural network with attention module for the task of classifying the tumor grade (LGG/HGG) in cropped multi-modal MR images. We adapt the architecture proposed in [13] and extend it to a multi-channel input. The network is trained on cropped T2-w, FLAIR and

T1-ce images, as these contain the most relevant information for differentiation between the tumor grades. In addition, we utilize the generated synthetic data to introduce more variation to the training and handle the problem of limited data. The trained classification model is evaluated on the same test set used for evaluating the segmentation performance, achieving an accuracy of 97.55% and 93.55% for identifying the HGG and LGG tumors, respectively. In comparison, a baseline model, trained without synthetic data augmentation achieves, an accuracy of 91.78% and 85.41% for classifying HGG and LGG tumors, respectively.

2.4 Fine-Grained Brain Tumor Region Segmentation

Once the tumor area is identified through the procedure in Sect. 2.2, the cropped MRIs are used to segment the three tumor subregions. We utilize the same network as for the whole-tumor segmentation (Fig. 4), with a few minor adjustments. We treat this task as a multi-class segmentation problem, where we utilize the sum of Dice and cross-entropy loss, which operates on the three class labels (edema, necrosis and enhancing tumor). To boost the performance of the model and improve its generalization capabilities, we add synthetic images generated in Sect. 2.1 to the real training data. We synthesize HGG and LGG images using 5 label deformations per original label image, using 100 HGG and 30 LGG original labels, for a total of 500 HGG images added to the training of the HGG segmentaion model, **M_Syn_HGG**, and a total of 150 synthetic LGG images for training the LGG segmentation model, **M_Syn_LGG**. Note that all synthetic images are cropped around the region of interest (the tumor area).

As a post-processing step, besides connected component analysis, we remove the false positive predictions of the enhancing tumor in cases when the predictions are below a certain threshold and replace them by the necrotic tissue.

3 Results and Discussion

3.1 Material

We develop and evaluate the proposed pipeline using the BraTS2020 training data [1], consisting of 369 multi-institutional pre-operative multi-modal MRI HGG (N = 293) and LGG (LN = 76) scans. Ground truth annotations consist of the enhancing tumor (ET), peritumoral edema (ED), necrotic and non-enhancing tumor (NCR/NET) [8]. All data is registered and skull-stripped. A summary of data utilization is shown in Table 1. It is important to note that the data used for training the conditional GAN (CGAN) differs from the data used for synthesis, as well as from the data utilized for training of segmentation and classification modules. Moreover, the testing is performed on data completely unseen throughout the whole training and generation pipeline. We additionally evaluate the trained models on 125 unseen images from the BraTS2020 validation set[1].

---

[1] https://ipp.cbica.upenn.edu/.

Table 1. Summary of dataset used for conditional image synthesis and segmentation.

Brats2020 challenge dataset [2]			
No. of Images	369	**Data distribution**	293 HGG/76 LGG
Matrix size	$240 \times 240 \times 155$	**CGAN Training**	100 HGG/30 LGG
Resolution	$1 \times 1 \times 1$ mm^3	**CGAN Synthesis**	153 HGG/30 LGG
Tumor grade	HGG, LGG	**Seg/Class Training**	160 HGG/60 LGG
Contrast	T1, T2, T1ce, FLAIR	**Seg/Class Testing**	33 HGG/16 LGG

3.2   Experimental Setup

We compare the proposed approach, consisting of separately trained segmentation models for HGG and LGG data (**M_Syn_HGG** and **M_Syn_LGG**), additionally augmented with the generated synthetic data to models trained only on real HGG and LGG images (**M_HGG** and **M_LGG**), available in the BraTS2020 training set. In addition, we train a heterogeneous model on mixed real LGG and HGG images, **M_HGG_LGG**, to showcase the benefit of stratifying training data by tumor grade groups. Finally, we evaluate the complete pipeline (**M_Ours**) on the BraTS2020 validation data and compare it to the performance of the baseline **M_HGG_LGG** model, which does not include any additional modules from the proposed pipeline (tumor detection, classification and augmentation with generated synthetic images).

3.3   Evaluation

The evaluation of the proposed method is performed on the enhancing tumor (ET), tumor core (TC; union of NCR/NET and ET) and whole tumor (WT; union of NCR/NET, ET and ED) in terms of average Dice scores, 95th percentile Hausdorff distances (HD95), sensitivity and precision. The performance of HGG and LGG models on HGG and LGG images, respectively, is shown in Fig. 5 in terms of average Dice and HD scores. We observe that the addition of synthetic data has significantly improved the segmentation performance for both HGG and LGG test cases across all tumor sub-regions (for $p<0.01$ according to the Wilcoxon signed-rank test). This is particularly notable for models trained and evaluated on LGG data, as the number of LGG images in the dataset used is limited. More detailed results are shown in Table 2, where we additionally report sensitivity and precision, computed only on the brain region. We notice the improvement in segmentation performance across all metrics, whereby most falsely classified regions belong to the enhancing tumor region and tumor core (for LGG images). It is interesting to note that the **M_HGG** model performs consistently better than the model trained with mixed LGG and HGG images, which indicates that the stratified approach towards training with a large enough and variable training set could be significantly more robust compared to standard ad hoc training approaches with all available data. This does not apply to the

M_LGG model, which we hypothesize is mainly due to a small training set (N = 60). In general, we observe an improvement in segmentation performance by utilizing the stratified training approach in combination with synthetic data in up to 85% of test cases, with up to 55% of cases exhibiting an improvement by more than 5% in Dice score. In addition, up to 40% of cases exhibit an improvement by more than 10% in Dice sore. Similar behaviour is observed by evaluating the proposed pipeline on the unseen validation data from the BraTS2020 Challenge, as seen in Table 3.

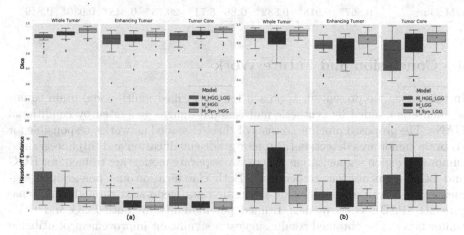

Fig. 5. Average Dice and Hausdorff Distance scores across three different tumor regions, evaluated on (a) HGG images and (b) LGG images. All results obtained by models **M_Syn_HGG** and **M_Syn_LGG** are statistically significant (p<0.01) compared to the other two models, according to the Wilcoxon signed-rank test.

Table 2. Performance of models trained with LGG and HGG data (**M_Syn_HGG**), models trained on stratified data (**M_HGG** and **M_LGG**) and stratified models trained with the addition of synthetic data (**M_Syn_HGG** and **M_Syn_LGG**.

HGG Tumors (Test set, N = 33)											
Model	Dice			HD95 (pix)			Sensitivity			Precision		
	WT	ET	TC	WT	ET	TC	WT	ET	TC	WT	ET	TC
M_HGG_LGG	0.907	0.880	0.893	28.18	13.05	15.22	0.916	0.845	0.873	0.931	0.941	0.932
M_HGG	0.925	0.893	0.922	22.11	8.96	9.65	0.922	0.858	0.909	0.947	0.955	0.943
M_Syn_HGG	**0.952**	**0.924**	**0.949**	**12.09**	**6.59**	**6.41**	**0.943**	**0.896**	**0.928**	**0.960**	**0.977**	**0.976**
LGG Tumors (Test set, N = 16)											
M_HGG_LGG	0.834	0.735	0.683	36.99	17.96	30.83	0.810	0.799	0.849	0.839	0.832	0.770
M_LGG	0.817	0.692	0.729	48.22	21.97	35.03	0.787	0.732	0.858	0.843	0.829	0.715
M_Syn_LGG	**0.895**	**0.836**	**0.856**	**18.01**	**11.80**	**18.09**	**0.853**	**0.818**	**0.879**	**0.881**	**0.847**	**0.801**

Table 3. Performance of the proposed pipeline (**M_Ours**) against the baseline **M_HGG_LGG** model on BRATS2020 validation set. * represents values significantly higher compared to the baseline, according to the Wilcoxon signed-rank test for $p < 0.01$.

BraTS2020 validation set (N = 125)									
Model	Dice			HD95 (pixels)			Recall		
	TC	WT	ET	TC	WT	ET	TC	WT	ET
M_HGG_LGG	0.817	0.878	0.775	7.79	8.83	31.35	0.797	0.907	0.719
M_Ours	0.867*	0.918*	0.832*	6.86	5.71*	20.73*	0.848*	0.936*	0.819*

4   Conclusion and Future Work

In this paper, we present an approach for a stratified multi-modal brain tumor segmentation, aided by synthetic multi-modal images generated by conditional GANs. The proposed pipeline consists of three cascaded networks, responsible for (i) brain tumor area detection (ii) tumor grade classification and (iii) fine-grained tumor sub-region segmentation, where two separate models are trained, for HGG and LGG segmentation, respectively. Both classification and fine-grained segmentation networks are aided by synthetic data, generated through four separate 2D SPADE GAN models, trained per modality for both LGG and HGG tumor types. The obtained results suggest a significant improvement of utilizing both the stratified approach to training, as well as synthetic data, especially in cases where data is limited. In future work, we plan to extend the analysis to larger and more variable training and testing sets and incorporate an additional segmentation model trained on both HGG and LGG images for ambiguously classified tumors. On the other hand, evaluating the performance of each stratified model on a miss-classified tumor type (e.g. the M_HGG evaluated on LGG tumors) could be beneficial for gaining a further insight into types of features captured by these models and their capability to differentiate between tumor grades. Finally, we plan to investigate adversarial and multi-task approaches to combine the tasks of classification and segmentation.

Acknowledgements. This research is part of the openGTN project, supported by the European Union in the Marie Curie Innovative Training Networks (ITN) fellowship program under project No. 764465.

References

1. Bakas, S., et al.: Advancing the cancer genome atlas glioma mri collections with expert segmentation labels and radiomic features. Sci. Data **4**(1), 1–13 (2017)
2. Bakas, S., et al.: Identifying the best machine learning algorithms for brain tumor segmentation, progression assessment, and overall survival prediction in the brats challenge. arXiv preprint arXiv:1811.02629 (2018)

3. Bauer, S., Wiest, R., Nolte, L.P., Reyes, M.: A survey of mri-based medical image analysis for brain tumor studies. Phys. Med. Biol. **58**(13), R97 (2013)
4. Brosch, T., Saalbach, A.: Foveal fully convolutional nets for multi-organ segmentation. In: Medical Imaging 2018: Image Processing, vol. 10574, p. 105740U. International Society for Optics and Photonics (2018)
5. Chen, L.C., Papandreou, G., Kokkinos, I., Murphy, K., Yuille, A.L.: Deeplab: Semantic image segmentation with deep convolutional nets, atrous convolution, and fully connected crfs. IEEE Trans. Pattern Anal. Mach. Intell. **40**(4), 834–848 (2017)
6. Kamnitsas, K., et al.: Efficient multi-scale 3D CNN with fully connected CRF for accurate brain lesion segmentation. Med. Image Anal. **36**, 61–78 (2017)
7. Li, X., Chen, H., Qi, X., Dou, Q., Fu, C.W., Heng, P.A.: H-DenseUNet: hybrid densely connected UNet for liver and tumor segmentation from CT volumes. IEEE Trans. Med. Imaging **37**(12), 2663–2674 (2018)
8. Menze, B.H., et al.: The multimodal brain tumor image segmentation benchmark (brats). IEEE Trans. Med. Imaging **34**(10), 1993–2024 (2014)
9. Park, T., Liu, M.Y., Wang, T.C., Zhu, J.Y.: Semantic image synthesis with spatially-adaptive normalization. In: Proceedings of the IEEE/CVF Conference on Computer Vision and Pattern Recognition, pp. 2337–2346 (2019)
10. Pereira, S., Pinto, A., Alves, V., Silva, C.A.: Brain tumor segmentation using convolutional neural networks in mri images. IEEE Trans. Med. Imaging **35**(5), 1240–1251 (2016)
11. Rebsamen, M., Knecht, U., Reyes, M., Wiest, R., Meier, R., McKinley, R.: Divide and conquer: stratifying training data by tumor grade improves deep learning-based brain tumor segmentation. Front. Neurosci. **13**, 1182 (2019)
12. Ronneberger, O., Fischer, P., Brox, T.: U-Net: Convolutional networks for biomedical image segmentation. In: Navab, N., Hornegger, J., Wells, W.M., Frangi, A.F. (eds.) MICCAI 2015. LNCS, vol. 9351, pp. 234–241. Springer, Cham (2015). https://doi.org/10.1007/978-3-319-24574-4_28
13. Zhang, J., Zheng, B., Gao, A., Feng, X., Liang, D., Long, X.: A 3d densely connected convolution neural network with connection-wise attention mechanism for Alzheimer's disease classification. Magn. Reson. Imaging **78**, 119–126 (2021)

Efficient Medical Image Assessment via Self-supervised Learning

Chun-Yin Huang[1(✉)], Qi Lei[2], and Xiaoxiao Li[1(✉)]

[1] University of British Columbia, Vancouver, Canada
{chunyinh,xiaoxiao.li}@ece.ubc.ca
[2] Princeton University, Princeton, USA
qilei@princeton.edu

Abstract. High-performance deep learning methods typically rely on large annotated training datasets, which are difficult to obtain in many clinical applications due to the high cost of medical image labeling. Existing data assessment methods commonly require knowing the labels in advance, which are not feasible to achieve our goal of *'knowing which data to label.'* To this end, we formulate and propose a novel and efficient data assessment strategy, **EX**ponenti**A**l Marginal s**IN**gular valu**E** (EXAMINE) score, to rank the quality of unlabeled medical image data based on their useful latent representations extracted via Self-supervised Learning (SSL) networks. Motivated by theoretical implication of SSL embedding space, we leverage a Masked Autoencoder [8] for feature extraction. Furthermore, we evaluate data quality based on the marginal change of the largest singular value after excluding the data point in the dataset. We conduct extensive experiments on a pathology dataset. Our results indicate the effectiveness and efficiency of our proposed methods for selecting the most valuable data to label.

1 Introduction

Artificial intelligence (AI) such as deep learning has became a powerful tool for medical image analysis. Its success relies on the availability of abundant high quality dataset. However, medical images collected from different sources vary in their quality due to the various imaging devices, protocols and techniques. When trained with low-quality data, AI models can be compromised. Furthermore, labeling medical images for AI training requires domain experts and is usually costly and time consuming. Therefore, it is demanding to have an automated framework to effectively assess and screen data quality before data labeling and model training.

There are numerous definitions of data quality. Data is generally considered to be of high quality if "fit for [its] intended uses in operations, decision making and planning" [4,5,16]. In the context of training an AI predictive model, good data are the fuel of AI. Namely, data with better quality can help obtain higher prediction accuracy. However, how to quantitatively assess data's quality for AI tasks is under-explored. Previous works [6,10] mainly propose to estimate data values in the context of supervised machine learning, which requires knowledge

H. V. Nguyen et al. (Eds.): DALI 2022, LNCS 13567, pp. 102–111, 2022.
https://doi.org/10.1007/978-3-031-17027-0_11

of labels and repeated training of a target utility. Such setting lacks practical value as data labels are typically not available at the data preparation stage for data privacy, labeling cost, and computational efficiency concerns. Differently, we aim to develop a cost-effective scheme for data assessment in the context of unsupervised learning to tackle the limitations of the existing methods, in which no labeling is required during assessment.

A trending and powerful unsupervised representation learning strategy is self-supervised learning (SSL). SSL solves auxiliary pretext tasks without requiring labeled data to learn useful semantic representations. These pretext tasks are created solely using the input features, such as predicting a missing image patch [8], recovering the color channels of an image from context [19], predicting missing words in texts [12], forcing the similarity of the different views of images [1,7], etc. Motivated by the recent discovery that SSL could embed data into linearly separable representations under proper data assumptions [13,17], we show that 'good' and 'bad' data can be distinguished by examining the change of the data representation matrices' singular value by removing a certain data point.

In this work, we tackle a practically demanding yet challenging problem—medical image assessment (also referred as data assessment in this work). To this end, we develop a novel and efficient pipeline for medical image assessment *without knowing data labels*. As shown in Fig. 1, we propose a new metric, **EX**ponenti**A**l Marginal s**IN**ular valu**E** (EXAMINE) score to evaluate the value (or referred as quality) of individual data by first using SSL to extract the features, and then calculate the value of the data using Singular Value Decomposition (SVD). EXAMINE scores are useful in indicating the essential data to be annotated, which can not only abundantly reduce the effort in manual labeling but also mitigate the negative effect of mislabeled data, and further improve the target model. Our chief contributions are summarized as follows:

- We are the first to show the feasibility of using an unsupervised learning framework to assess medical data by utilizing SSL and SVD, which is a more cost-efficient and practical method to evaluate data compared to previous work.
- EXAMINE can assess data *without* knowing the label, which reduces annotation efforts and the chance of mislabeling.
- We conduct experiments on the simulated medical dataset to demonstrate the feasibility of using EXAMINE scores to distinguish data with different qualities and show comparable performance to previous supervised learning based works.

2 Preliminaries

2.1 Supervised-Learning-Based Data Assessment

The goal of data assessment is using a valuation function to map an input data to a single value that indicate its quality. Supervised-learning-based data assessments assume knowing a labeled dataset $\mathcal{N}^l = \{(x_i, y_i) | i \in [N], x_i \in \mathcal{X}, y_i \in \mathcal{Y}\}$ where N is the number of the labeled data, an utility model $f : \mathcal{N}^l \mapsto \mathcal{Y}$, a held-out labeled testing set $\mathcal{N}^t = \{(x_i', y_i')| i \in [M], x_i' \in \mathcal{X}, y_i' \in \mathcal{Y}\}$ where M is the number of the testing data, and a value function $V : (f, \mathcal{N}^l, \mathcal{N}^t) \mapsto \mathbb{R}$ (e.g., the accuracy of $\mathcal{N}^t$ evaluated by f that is trained on $\mathcal{N}^l$). The simplest assessment metric is by performing leave-one-out (LOO) on the training set and calculating the performance differences on the testing set. The i-th data samples value is defined as:

$$\phi_i^{\text{LOO}} = V_f(\mathcal{N}^l) - V_f(\mathcal{N}^l \backslash \{i\}). \tag{1}$$

A more advanced but computational costly approach is Data Shapley [6]. Shapley value for data valuation resembles a game where training data points are the players and the payoff is defined by the goodness of fit achieved by a model on the testing data. Given a subset S, let $f_S(\cdot)$ be a model trained on S. Then Shapley value of a data point $(x_i, y_i) \in \mathcal{N}$ is defined as:

$$\phi_i^{\text{SHAP}} = \sum_{S \subseteq \mathcal{N} \backslash \{x_i\}} \frac{V_f(S \cup \{x_i\}) - V_f(S)}{\binom{|\mathcal{N}^l| - 1}{|S|}}, \tag{2}$$

where $V_f(S)$ is the performance of the utility model f trained on subset S of the data. Suppose each training of f takes time T, the computational complexity of Eq. (1) and Eq. (2) is $\mathcal{O}(TN)$ and $\mathcal{O}(T2^N)$[1], respectively. Also, training a deep utility function (*e.g.*, neural networks) leads to a large T.

2.2   Formulation of Unsupervised-Learning-Based Data Assessment

Motivation story Labeling is costly and time consuming in many medical imaging tasks. AI developers may want to pay for labeling some data points to train a particular machine learning model. In such a scenario, supervised-learning-based methods (Sect. 2.1) cannot fulfill the aim. Therefore, algorithms that can automatically identify low quality data before labeling data are highly desired.

To address computational issue and demand for task/label-agnostic data quality, we propose to conduct quantitative data quality assessment via unsupervised learning. Different from the formulations of LOO (Eq. (1)) and Shapley value (Eq. (2)), here we propose a new problem formulation to infer i-th data's quality by assigning it a value $\phi_i : (\mathcal{X}, i) \mapsto \mathbb{R}$ using unlabeled data only.

3   Our Method

3.1   Theoretical Implication

Our proposed EXAMINE is well motivated by representation theory of SSL. We start by restating Theorem 1 proved in [13] that under proper assumptions, the embedded space obtained by the reconstruction-based SSL strategy forms a linearly separable space of the embedded feature and a related task. Then, *Remark* 1 presents how we use Theorem 1 to guide the design of EXAMINE.

---

[1] In practice, there are approximation methods for calculating Shapley value, but the it still requires around $\mathcal{O}(T\text{poly}(N))$ [11].

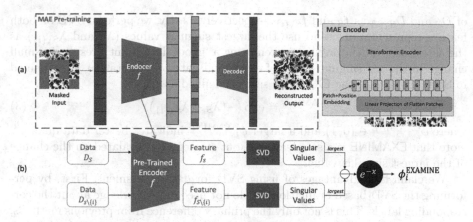

Fig. 1. Proposed pipeline for EXAMINE data assessment. (a) Using the state-of-the art reconstruction-based SSL strategy, MAE [8] architecture for pre-training an rep-resentation extractor (encoder). (b) EXAMINE first utilizes the pre-trained encoder to extract semantic features f_S and $f_{S\setminus\{i\}}$ from input data D_S and $D_{S\setminus\{i\}}$, where $D_{S\setminus\{i\}}$ denotes input data D_S *without* data point i. The features then pass the SVD module to find the largest singular values λ_S and $\lambda_{S\setminus\{i\}}$. The EXAMINE score of data point i is defined as Eq. (3).

Theorem 1 (informal [13]). *For two views of a data $X_1, X_2 \in \mathcal{X}$ and their classification label $Y \in \mathbb{R}^k$. Under the class conditional independence assumption, i.e., $X_1 \perp X_2|Y$, for some $w \in \mathbb{R}^{m \times k}$ the representation $\psi^* : \mathcal{X} \mapsto \mathbb{R}^m$ that minimizes a reconstruction loss $\mathcal{L}(\psi) = \mathbb{E}_{(X_1, X_2)}\left[\|X_1 - \psi(X_2)\|^2\right]$ satisfies*

$$w^\top \psi^*(X_1) = \mathbb{E}[Y|X_1].$$

Remark 1. Theorem 1 indicates two desired properties with 'good' data that (approximately) satisfy class-conditional independence. First, the data will have a good geometric property in the learned representation space, namely they become clusters that are (almost) linearly separable (by w). Second, the learned representation has *variance (top singular value of its covariance matrix)* controlled by that of $\mathbb{E}[Y|X_1]$, which is very **small** (since the label is almost determined entirely by the image itself). Such properties on the reconstruction-based SSL embedding space are not satisfied for 'bad' data. Therefore when observing data X_1 is noisy or with low quality, $\psi^*(X_1)$ tends to have higher variance.

3.2 Data Assessment on Singular Value

As shown in the Fig. 1(b), to assess data from a dataset $D_S \in R^{N \times C}$, where N is the number of data and C is the dimension of data, we denote the dataset without i-th data point as $D_{S\setminus\{i\}} \in R^{(N-1) \times C}$. To begin with, we employ SSL and the unlabeled data to train an encoder that is able to extract the low-dimensional semantic information. We denote the representation of the SSL embedding space of D_S and $D_{S\backslash\{i\}}$ as f_S and $f_{S\backslash\{i\}}$, respectively. Lastly, we perform SVD on both feature representations, and use the largest singular values (λ_S and $\lambda_{S\backslash\{i\}}$) as the assessment indicator, that is, removing a 'good' data point i results in small change in the top singular value of embedded data representation f (explained in Sect. 3.1). Thus, the EXAMINE score is defined as

$$\phi_i^{\text{EXAMINE}} = \exp\left(-(\lambda_S - \lambda_{S\backslash\{i\}})\right), \tag{3}$$

where $\phi_i^{\text{EXAMINE}} \in (0,1)$ and a larger ϕ_i^{EXAMINE} indicates better data quality[2]. Note that EXAMINE is also a leave-one-out strategy but evalated on the change of the largest singular value.

We claim two advantages of using SVD for data assessment. First, by performing the SVD-based evaluation, we do not need any knowledge about the corresponding labels. This is not only the primary difference from previous methods, but also a perfect fit to our problem set up - finding good data to be labeled. Second, unlike previous methods (i.e., LOO and Data Shapely, see Sect. 2.1) that rely on extensively training a new model for different data combinations, our proposed method is efficient by performing SVD once for each data point without additional model training after the SSL encoder has been trained offline.

3.3 Forming Embedding Space Using Masked Auto-encoding

As the raw medical images are high-dimensional and have spurious features (e.g., density, light, dose) that are irrelevant to their labels, directly applying SVD to them cannot capture task-related variance. Based on our theory developed on reconstruction-based SSL (Sect. 3.1), we utilize a state-of-the-art reconstructed-based strategy, Masked Auto-Encoder (MAE) [8] to learn lower-dimensional semantic feature embedding. As shown in Fig. 1(a), MAE utilizes state-of-the-art image classification framework, Vision Transformer (ViT) [3], as the encoder for semantic feature extraction, and uses a lighter version of ViT as decoder. It first divides an input image into patches, randomly blocks a certain percentage of image patches, and then feeds them into the autoencoder architecture. By blocking out a large amount of image patches, the model is forced to learn a more complete representation. With the aim of positional embedding and transformer architecture, MAE is able to generalize the relationship between each image patch and obtain the semantic information among the whole image, which achieves the state-of-the-art performance in self-supervised image representation training. *This also reduces the correlation between spurious features and labels*, compared to the traditional dimension reduction methods [2].

4 Experiment

4.1 Experiment Setup and Dataset

We evaluate EXAMINE on a binary classification task for PCam [18], a microscopic dataset (image size 96×96) for identifying metastatic tissue in histopathologic scans of lymph node sections. Since noise is usually the main corruption in

---

[2] $\lambda_S > \lambda_{S\backslash\{i\}}$ is for sure given the properties of singular value.

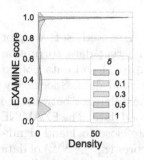

(a) EXAMINE with MAE

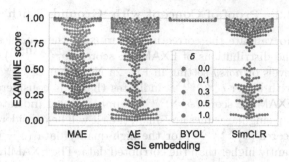

(b) Comparison with different embedding

Fig. 2. Proof of concept and comparison with baseline embedding methods. Observe that EXAMINE scores (ϕ_i^{EXAMINE}) get lower when noise level increases (a), and the EXAMINE scores (ϕ_i^{EXAMINE}) in (b) shows that reconstrucion-based SSL methods perform better in separating different noise levels.

medical images, we add non-zero mean Gaussian noise to a portion of the data to simulate real world scenario.

We split the dataset into four disjoint sets following the scale of [6]:

- **SSL Pre-Training Set** and **Assessed Set**: 160,000 and 500 unlabeled data points randomly sampled from PCam, respectively. We add 4 different level ($\mathcal{N}(\delta, \delta \times m)$, where m is the mean of the dataset and $\delta = \{0.1, 0.3, 0.5, 1\}$) of noise to 60000 data points of **SSL Pre-Training Set** and 400 data points in **Assessed Set**.
- **Clean Train Set** and **Validation Set**: 100 and 20,000 labeled data points randomly sampled from PCam. They are used to validate the data selection in an example downstream task after obtaining EXAMINE scores (ϕ_i^{EXAMINE}).

The experiments are run on NVIDIA DeForce RTX 3090 Graphics card with PyTorch. For MAE training, we select Cosine Annealing LR scheduler [14] and AdamW LR optimizer [15] with weight decay 0.05 and momentum $\{0.9, 0.95\}$. We train MAE for 200 epochs using batch size 256 ,and set image size 72, patch size 8, masking ratio 40%. As indicated in [1,7,8] that SSL training requires a large amount of data, we begin with training a MAE on **SSL Pre-Training Set**. To ensure the training stability, we first train MAE without any noisy data, and finetune it afterward. This step is to distinguish our setting from detection out of distribution samples. After pretraining the MAE encoder, we use the frozen encoder layers as our backbone to extract the low dimensional representations. All of our experiments are repeated five times with different random seeds and we report the mean value of the five trials.

4.2   Proof of Concept with 'Ground-Truth'

To validate the correctness of ranking the samples in **Assessed Set**, we plot the distributions of EXAMINE scores (ϕ_i^{EXAMINE}) at different data corruption levels of *noisy* setting in Fig. 2a Note that $\phi_i^{\text{EXAMINE}} \in (0, 1)$ and data point i with larger ϕ_i^{EXAMINE} indicates that it is considered a good data. Specifically, EXAMINE score (ϕ_i^{EXAMINE}) approaching 1 indicates the difference between the top singular values are small, thus it will be considered good data. The EXAMINE scores (ϕ_i^{EXAMINE}) for the high-quality data ($\delta = 0$) are close to 1 and significantly higher than the corrupted data. The EXAMINE scores (ϕ_i^{EXAMINE}) of data with low-level corruption ($\delta = 0.5$) are also separable from those with high-level corruption($\delta = 1$).

4.3   Comparison with Alternative Embedding Methods

We investigate the alternative feature encoders and compare their performance with MAE. Specifically, we replace MAE with SimCLR [1] and BYOL [7], two alternative SSL algorithms, and Autoencoder (AE) [9], a naïve reconstruction-based embedding strategy. SimCLR learns embedding by enforcing the closeness of an image and its augmented views while enlarging the distance from other images in the dataset (or batch). BYOL regularizes the multi-views of an image without sampling negative samples by training two similar networks (the online network and the target network) simultaneously. We use the same strategy as training MAE for these alternative encoders. Figure 2b shows that using MAE embedding to calculate EXAMINE scores (ϕ_i^{EXAMINE}) provides the best separability for the clean data from the corrupted data. The reason is that MAE best satisfies the theoretical conditions that support our proposal (Theorem 1). AE is second to MAE, but separation boundaries are less clear.

4.4   Comparison with Baseline Data Valuation Methods

We compare EXAMINE with supervised data valuation methods, LOO (Eq. 1 and Truncated Monte Carlo (TMC) version of Data Shapley (Eq. 2) [6], as well as a baseline method that randomly assigns data values. All these methods are applied on **Assessed Set**'s features extracted by the pre-trained MAE. We design four experiments to evaluate how selecting data using the different data assessment methods can affect the classification accuracy. We report the averaged test accuracy on **Validation Set** using logistic regression models (LRM).

Figures 3a and 3b show the results of adding data for training. We start with a LRM trained on the small **Clean Training Set**, and then add good/bad data from **Assessed Set** following the descending/ascending orders of their data values. Our results show that adding data with high EXAMINE score (ϕ_i^{EXAMINE}) achieves comparable accuracy curve as Data Shapley, while adding data with low EXAMINE scores (ϕ_i^{EXAMINE}) results in similar curve as Data Shapley in the beginning and overall lies in between Data Shapley and LOO. This indicates that EXAMINE score (ϕ_i^{EXAMINE}) is able to identify what data to be labeled and

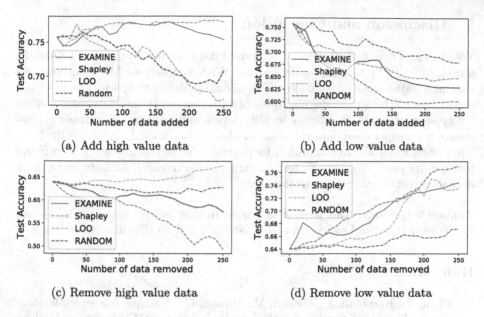

(a) Add high value data   (b) Add low value data

(c) Remove high value data   (d) Remove low value data

Fig. 3. Comparison with baseline data valuation methods. Adding good data(a) and removing bad data(d) should increase accuracy. Adding bad data(b) and removing good data(c) should result in accuracy drop. We conclude that EXAMINE can help model training by identifying good and bad data.

added to training set. Figures 3c and 3d show the results of removing data for training. We first train LRM on **Assessed Set**, and then remove good/bad data following the descending/ascending orders of their data values. Our result shows that removing high/low EXAMINE score ($\phi_i^{\mathrm{EXAMINE}}$) data results in accuracy curve that is slightly worse than Data Shapley. We would like to emphasize Data Shapley uses utility function which requires labels to determine the data value, while EXAMINE score ($\phi_i^{\mathrm{EXAMINE}}$) is calculated only on data itself, which is more efficient in real-world scenario. Overall, EXAMINE shows comparable(or at best slightly worser) data assessment performance to Data Shapley *without* knowing the labels of the data.

In addition to successfully providing correct inspection on data quality, our method significantly reduces the computational cost without requiring training utility functions. The running time to obtain the data values using EXAMINE, LOO, and TMC Data Shapley for the whole **Assessed Set** under our experiment setting are 23 s, 10 min, and 460 min, respectively[3].

---

[3] The running time for LOO and Data Shapley can significantly increase if we use a deep neural network as the utility model.

5 Discussion and Conclusion

We present a new and efficient unsupervised data evaluation method, EXAMINE scores ϕ_i^{EXAMINE}, to assess data quality. With the help of MAE encoder, we can map data to the provable low-dimensional embedding space. The marginal differences on the largest singular value of data representation matrices can effectively separate data at different quality levels and achieve comparable performance with supervised data valuation methods when considering a specific task. This work takes a novel approach to promote AI in healthcare by identifying low quality data. We plan to test on larger scale medical datasets and collect domain experts' evaluations in the future.

Acknowledgement. This work is supported in part by the Natural Sciences and Engineering Research Council of Canada (NSERC) and NVIDIA Hardware Award.

References

1. Chen, T., Kornblith, S., Norouzi, M., Hinton, G.: A simple framework for contrastive learning of visual representations. In: International Conference on Machine Learning, pp. 1597–1607. PMLR (2020)
2. Chen, Y., Wei, C., Kumar, A., Ma, T.: Self-training avoids using spurious features under domain shift. Adv. Neural Inf. Process. Syst. **33**, 21061–21071 (2020)
3. Dosovitskiy, A., et al.: An image is worth 16x16 words: transformers for image recognition at scale. arXiv preprint arXiv:2010.11929 (2020)
4. Fadahunsi, K.P., et al.: Protocol for a systematic review and qualitative synthesis of information quality frameworks in eHealth. BMJ Open **9**(3), e024722 (2019)
5. Fadahunsi, K.P., et al.: Information quality frameworks for digital health technologies: systematic review. J. Med. Internet Res. **23**(5), e23479 (2021)
6. Ghorbani, A., Zou, J.: Data shapley: equitable valuation of data for machine learning. In: Chaudhuri, K., Salakhutdinov, R. (eds.) Proceedings of the 36th International Conference on Machine Learning. Proceedings of Machine Learning Research, vol. 97, pp. 2242–2251. PMLR (2019)
7. Grill, J.B., e al.: Bootstrap your own latent-a new approach to self-supervised learning. Adv. Neural Inf. Process. Syst. **33**, 21271–21284 (2020)
8. He, K., Chen, X., Xie, S., Li, Y., Dollár, P., Girshick, R.: Masked autoencoders are scalable vision learners. In: Proceedings of the IEEE/CVF Conference on Computer Vision and Pattern Recognition, pp. 16000–16009 (2022)
9. Hinton, G.E., Salakhutdinov, R.R.: Reducing the dimensionality of data with neural networks. Science **313**(5786), 504–507 (2006)
10. Jia, R., et al.: Towards efficient data valuation based on the shapley value. In: The 22nd International Conference on Artificial Intelligence and Statistics, pp. 1167–1176. PMLR (2019)
11. Jia, R., Sun, X., Xu, J., Zhang, C., Li, B., Song, D.: An empirical and comparative analysis of data valuation with scalable algorithms (2019)
12. Kenton, J.D.M.W.C., Toutanova, L.K.: Bert: pre-training of deep bidirectional transformers for language understanding. In: Proceedings of naacL-HLT, pp. 4171–4186 (2019)

13. Lee, J.D., Lei, Q., Saunshi, N., Zhuo, J.: Predicting what you already know helps: provable self-supervised learning. Adv. Neural Inf. Process. Syst. **34** (2021)
14. Loshchilov, I., Hutter, F.: Sgdr: stochastic gradient descent with warm restarts. arXiv preprint arXiv:1608.03983 (2016)
15. Loshchilov, I., Hutter, F.: Decoupled weight decay regularization. arXiv preprint arXiv:1711.05101 (2017)
16. Redman, T.C.: Data Driven: Profiting from Your Most Important Business Asset. Harvard Business Press (2008)
17. Tosh, C., Krishnamurthy, A., Hsu, D.: Contrastive learning, multi-view redundancy, and linear models. In: Algorithmic Learning Theory, pp. 1179–1206. PMLR (2021)
18. Veeling, B.S., Linmans, J., Winkens, J., Cohen, T., Welling, M.: Rotation equivariant CNNs for digital pathology. In: Frangi, A.F., Schnabel, J.A., Davatzikos, C., Alberola-López, C., Fichtinger, G. (eds.) MICCAI 2018. LNCS, vol. 11071, pp. 210–218. Springer, Cham (2018). https://doi.org/10.1007/978-3-030-00934-2_24
19. Zhang, R., Isola, P., Efros, A.A.: Colorful image colorization. In: Leibe, B., Matas, J., Sebe, N., Welling, M. (eds.) ECCV 2016. LNCS, vol. 9907, pp. 649–666. Springer, Cham (2016). https://doi.org/10.1007/978-3-319-46487-9_40

Few-Shot Learning Geometric Ensemble for Multi-label Classification of Chest X-Rays

Dana Moukheiber[1]([envelope]), Saurabh Mahindre[2], Lama Moukheiber[1],
Mira Moukheiber[1], Song Wang[3], Chunwei Ma[2], George Shih[4], Yifan Peng[4],
and Mingchen Gao[2]

[1] Massachusetts Institute of Technology, Cambridge, MA, USA
danamouk@mit.edu
[2] University at Buffalo, The State University of New York, Buffalo, NY, USA
mgao8@buffalo.edu
[3] The University of Texas at Austin, Austin, TX, USA
[4] Weill Cornell Medicine, New York, NY, USA

Abstract. This paper aims to identify uncommon cardiothoracic diseases and patterns on chest X-ray images. Training a machine learning model to classify rare diseases with multi-label indications is challenging without sufficient labeled training samples. Our model leverages the information from common diseases and adapts to perform on less common mentions. We propose to use multi-label few-shot learning (FSL) schemes including neighborhood component analysis loss, generating additional samples using distribution calibration and fine-tuning based on multi-label classification loss. We utilize the fact that the widely adopted nearest neighbor-based FSL schemes like ProtoNet are Voronoi diagrams in feature space. In our method, the Voronoi diagrams in the features space generated from multi-label schemes are combined into our geometric DeepVoro Multi-label ensemble. The improved performance in multi-label few-shot classification using the multi-label ensemble is demonstrated in our experiments (The code is publicly available at https://github.com/Saurabh7/Few-shot-learning-multilabel-cxray).

Keywords: Few-shot learning · Multi-label image classification · Chest X-ray · Ensemble learning · Computational geometry

1 Introduction

The interpretation of thoracic diseases usually begins with screening, using chest X-rays before ordering various other routine diagnostic augmentations, such as

---

D. Moukheiber and S. Mahindre—Equal contributions.

Supplementary Information The online version contains supplementary material available at https://doi.org/10.1007/978-3-031-17027-0_12.

CT scans, laboratory tests, pulmonary function tests, and biopsies [17]. Chest X-rays are inexpensive, use low radiation dose, and are ubiquitous, making them useful in diagnosing cardiothoracic abnormalities. In recent years, studies have shown the competency of convolutional neural network (CNN) architectures in achieving high performance on 14 common classes for a multi-label classification task, and sometimes at a level exceeding radiologists [13,16,19]. However, no study has yet investigated the multi-label classification of uncommon cardiothoracic abnormalities in chest X-rays. Procuring large and high-quality chest X-ray images representative of infrequent diseases requires expert-generated annotations which is time-consuming, and resource-intensive. This can limit the application of medical image classification to support rare cardiothoracic diseases.

These challenges motivate us to develop an approach to address the multi-classification of rare cardiothoracic disease based on few-shot learning (FSL), which aims to generalize from abundant base samples to inadequate novel samples. FSL algorithms can be categorized into several types: metric-based [18], optimization-based [7], and transfer learning-based [21] approaches. Recently there has been work on different ensemble methods for FSL to further improve the performance. The EASY model [1] proposes the use of an ensemble of backbones along with a concatenation of features to show state-of-the-art performance on multi-class data-sets. The geometric mean of the probabilities as a means to ensemble models has also been shown to perform well [22]. Another geometric based method called DeepVoro [15] shows that many metric-based FSL algorithms essentially partition the feature space into a Voronoi Diagram (VD) [2]. For example, prototypical networks [18] learn the embeddings of class prototypes using the euclidean distance as a metric. The queries are then classified using their nearest neighbors to the class prototypes. DeepVoro also proposes to use Cluster-induced Voronoi Diagram (CIVD) that allows for multiple centers per Voronoi cell, making it the state-of-the-art FSL.

In this work, we propose DeepVoro Multi-label, a method that combines both parametric and non-parametric multi-label FSL methods to capture different identifying signals from chest X-rays. Our proposed method is able to combine diverse information from multiple models and provide better performance using only a few samples from previously unseen classes. To the best of our knowledge, this method is the first to realize the potential of FSL in multi-label image classification of rare cardiothoracic diseases in the application of chest X-ray images. Our major contributions are summarized as follows: (1) Introducing parametric and non-parametric multi-label classification methods for FSL on chest X-rays. This includes adapting the neighborhood component analysis loss to account for pairs of samples with either multiple matching labels or zero matching labels, and altering the mean and covariance in the distribution calibration (DC) model to include all positive labels for a given class inorder to establish a multivariate Gaussian distribution, as well as using the binary cross-entropy loss (BCE) to account for multi-label classification. (2) Introducing DeepVoro Multi-label, a novel model that employs softmax function for multi-label classification. This model combines the individual proposed methods using their underlying geometric structure and evaluates them for identification of less common conditions in chest X-rays through a FSL framework. (3) The labels of a set of less common diseases would be an addition of the widely used chest X-ray datasets.

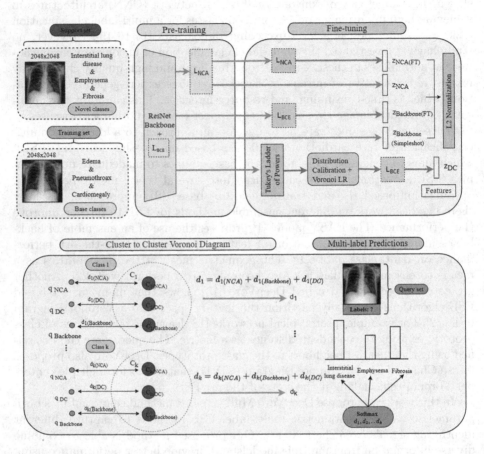

Fig. 1. Overview of the workflow of the proposed method.

2   Methods

The overall framework of our proposed approach is presented in Fig. 1. We propose a multi-label classification for uncommon cardiothoracic diseases on chest X-ray images. Our proposed method consists of three components: (1) pre-training a feature extractor (backbone) using a generic MIMIC-CXR imaging dataset with 14 common labels [11] to create a base subset for pre-training in a multi-label setting, (2) applying different schemes for few-shot learning on labeled support samples by sampling additional samples from calibrated distribution, using binary cross-entropy, and adapting neighborhood component analysis loss for multi-label chest X-ray images, and (3) combining these methods and their underlying Voronoi diagrams using a softmax function into our geometric DeepVoro Multi-label ensemble for evaluation on the query set.

Notation. We use $z = f_\Theta(x)$ to denote the features extracted from the final layer of the residual network for a sample x, where f_Θ denotes the pre-trained residual network backbone. While performing few-shot evaluation, support samples denote the seen (training) samples with novel classes, and query samples denote the unseen (test) samples.

Pre-training. We first train a residual network as a backbone for extracting features from the chest X-ray images. This backbone is responsible for learning various patterns and information from a large number of images available from the base classes. Residual networks [9] have been widely used for image classification and few-shot image classification on medical images [5]. We adopt a residual network architecture similar to [3,10] since it is suitable for the high dimensional nature of chest X-rays and the limitations of the hardware. The backbone is trained on the training set consisting of 14 base classes using a weighted binary cross-entropy loss. We introduced weights for each of the base classes to account for class imbalance present in the dataset.

$$L_{BCE} = - \sum_{i=1...n} \sum_{k=1...|C|} w_k y_{i_k} \log \hat{y_{i_k}} + (1 - y_{i_k}) \log (1 - \hat{y_{i_k}}) \qquad (1)$$

Few-Shot Learning. We adapt the pre-trained backbone to novel classes using various schemes described below. Finally, we combine the underlying Voronoi diagrams of these outputs geometrically into our DeepVoro Multi-label ensemble.

Fine-Tuning. The pre-trained backbone can be fine-tuned on the novel class support samples available. To perform fine-tuning, we replace the final classification layer with a layer where the number of neurons equals the number of novel classes. The BCE loss from Eq. 1 is used to fine-tune the model. This is labeled as Backbone (FT) in Fig. 1. We also directly use the features from the pretrained backbone without any fine-tuning since it has been shown to perform well on different multi-class classifications such as in simpleshot [21].

Neighborhood Component Analysis (NCA) can be used to learn embeddings of images where the distances between samples of the same classes are minimized and distances between samples of different classes are maximized [8,12]. We altered the NCA loss to extend to multi-label classification, wherein we minimize the distances between samples based on the number of positive labels that match those samples.

$$L_{NCA} = -\frac{1}{|B|} \sum_{i \in 1...b} \log \left(\frac{\sum_{\substack{j \in 1...b \\ i \neq j, n_{ij} > 0}} n_{ij} \, e^{-||z_i - z_j||^2}}{\sum_{\substack{j \in 1...b \\ i \neq j, n_{ij} > 0}} n_{ij} \, e^{-||z_i - z_j||^2} + \sum_{\substack{j \in 1...b \\ i \neq j, n_{ij} = 0}} e^{-||z_i - z_j||^2}} \right) \quad (2)$$

where $n_{ij} = \sum_{k \in 1...|C|} y_{ik}, y_{jk}$ is the number of matching positive labels between samples i and j and $||z_i - z_j||^2$ is euclidean distance between them. Thus we find an embedding where images with similar labels are closer by adding n_{ij} multiplier as a reward for matching samples to the numerator and penalizing the non-matching samples by adding their $e^{-||z_i - z_j||^2}$ term in the denominator. We use the loss from Eq. 2 to do additional pretraining and fine-tuning.

Sampling from Calibrated Distribution. Additional support samples can be introduced by sampling from a distribution calibrated using the statistics from base classes [23]. For each support sample available, a mean and variance value is calibrated from the nearest n base classes. The nearest n base classes are determined based on the base class statistics: mean μ_k and covariance Σ_k.

We define the calculation of means and covariance for base classes as described in Eq. (3). Here, we adapted the calculation to extend to a multi-label setting by using all samples with a positive label ($y_k = 1$) for class k to calculate the mean and covariance for that class. The calibrated mean and covariance value is then used to establish a multivariate Gaussian distribution from which additional samples are obtained.

$$\mu_k = \frac{\sum_{\substack{j=1...n_k \\ y_k=1}} z_j}{n_k}, \quad \Sigma_k = \frac{1}{n_k - 1} \sum_{\substack{j=1...n_k \\ y_k=1}} (z_j - \mu_k)(z_j - \mu_k)^T \quad (3)$$

DC (Voronoi-LR). The original and additional support samples are used to train a logistic regression (LR) classifier. We use the same BCE loss described in Eq. 1 to account for multi-label setting. In order to integrate this classifier in our geometric DeepVoro Multi-label ensemble, the classifier was modified as described in [15], wherein we restrict the bias term of the classifier to $\frac{1}{4}||W||_2^2$ and use $\frac{1}{2}W_k$ as the center for class k [14]. Using this modification, the underlying geometrical structure of LR (Power diagram) is reduced to a Voronoi diagram. This modified classifier is labeled as DC (Voronoi-LR) in Fig. 1.

Finally, we generate features using the schemes defined above for samples from novel classes and normalize them using the L2-norm [21]. The prototype for each scheme i and class k is calculated by averaging all support samples with label $y_k = 1$. This means that due to the multi-label setting, one sample can contribute to multiple prototypes. For generating an Area Under the Curve (AUC) performance of individual Voronoi diagram schemes, we used *soft nearest neighbor classification*, i.e., assign probability based on soft-max of distances to class prototypes.

DeepVoro Multi-label. Establishing cluster-to-cluster relationships for feature space subdivision has been proven effective for FSL based on Cluster-to-Cluster Voronoi Diagram (CCVD) [15]. Here we propose to use the features generated by simpleshot, DC (Vornoi-LR), Backbone fine-tuned on novel classes, and NCA loss to establish prototypes for each class. The influence function for the cluster-to-cluster relationship is defined as follows between an ordered set of prototypes for class k (C_k) and features for a sample z ($C(z)$). The α in the influence function is set to 1. The influence function calculates the sum of distances between feature and corresponding prototypes for models $i = 1, ..., |C|$ used in our DeepVoro Multi-label ensemble.

$$F(C_k, C(z)) = -sign(\alpha) \sum_{i=1...|C|} ||c_k^i - z_i||^{2\alpha} \tag{4}$$

Finally, instead of using an arg-max function for multi-class classification as proposed by DeepVoro [14], we use a soft-max function for a multi-label classification to obtain the final probability of a sample, z, lying in cell r_k for class k.

$$r(z)_k = \frac{\exp -F(C_k, C(z))}{\sum_{k'=1...|C|} \exp -F(C_{k'}, C'(z))} \tag{5}$$

3 Experiments

3.1 Dataset

We conduct experiments using our proposed framework on a generic chest X-ray dataset, MIMIC-CXR [11] which comprises 377,110 high-resolution frontal and lateral chest X-ray images and provides 14 common cardiothoracic labels with corresponding free-text radiology reports. For pre-training the 14 common base classes, we use 248,020 frontal chest X-rays with Posterior-Anterior (PA) and Anterior Posterior (AP) views. We utilize RadText, an efficient automated radiology report analysis system pipeline [20] that offers a rule-based named entity recognition method to combine information from terminological resources and characteristics of the disease classes of interest, to extract the assertion status of five less common novel classes. Table 1 shows the frequency of the uncommon novel labels in the reports that fall into a group of diseases or findings categories. A synonym vocabulary for each novel class is constructed by consulting radiologists and using RadLex search engine tool. These vocabularies are utilized by the named entity recognition module and the assertion status of these recognized named entities are identified in the negation/uncertainty detection module of the pipeline.

3.2 Baselines

We compare the DeepVoro Multi-label model against: 1) **Backbone (FT) classification** We use the final fully connected layer of the backbone pre-trained on

Table 1. Frequency of positive labels in MIMIC-CXR on 24,384 unique radiologic studies with one or more novel classes. (% of the label mentions across 24,384 studies.)

Novel Classes	Frequency
Chronic obstructive pulmonary disease	5063 (20.7%)
Emphysema	5216 (21.4%)
Interstitial lung disease	1070 (4.4%)
Calcification	14075 (57.7%)
Fibrosis	1025 (4.2%)

14 classes and fine-tuned on five classes to establish a simple classifier baseline. 2) **Simpleshot** [21] We implement the Voronoi diagram based method using features extracted from the pre-trained backbone with the modification of soft-nearest neighbor classification for multi-label setting.

3.3 Implementation Details

During data preprocessing, the input chest X-rays undergo minimal cropping to 2048×2048 dimensions. This is done to maintain the high resolution of x-rays and avoid information loss while detecting novel classes. We use a random rotation of $15°$ and color jitter during training time.

For pre-training, the backbone is implemented with a series of seven residual blocks [3,9], which results in an embedding in 2,048 dimension space. A fully connected layer is employed after the backbone to generate predictions for each of the 14 base classes. The positive weights are calculated as $w_k = \frac{\text{\# of no findings}}{\text{\# in class } k}$. The maximum positive weight is set to five. We use an Adam optimizer with a learning rate of 10^{-4} and weight decay of 10^{-4} to minimize the loss in 1. The mini-batch size is set to 32 due to hardware limitations, and we perform training on the whole training set for three epochs.

To evaluate few-shot novel classes, we generate episodes by uniformly sampling without replacement, chest X-ray images belonging to a particular novel class. In a m shot episode, $2m$ images are sampled with a positive label, $y_k = 1$ for each class k, wherein m images are used as support samples and the performance is evaluated on the remaining m query samples. There are N total classes. Then for each N-way m shot episode, we have Nm support images and Nm query images. We use AUC to compare the performance, a commonly used metric to assess the multi-label classification of chest X-rays [4]. DeepVoro Multi-label for 5-shot, 10-shot, and 50-shot is time efficient as it's a non-parametric method and no additional training is needed in the ensemble step. As seen in Supplement Section 1.1, the total time per episode across 5-shot, 10-shot and 50-shot is 259, 388 and 1340 respectively.

3.4   Results and Evaluation

In Table 2, we report the AUC performance on the novel classes. Before evaluation on the novel classes, to demonstrate the effectiveness of the pre-trained backbone performance on base classes we obtain the AUC for the residual network backbone trained on 14 base classes which is 0.785 on the test dataset. The baseline models including Backbone (FT) classification and Backbone VD (Simpleshot) are described in Sect. 3.2. The remaining four rows in Table 2, show the performance of individual Voronoi diagram based models. And, the final row presents the DeepVoro Multi-label model which combines the individual models geometrically. We can see a consistent improvement in the individual models compared to the baseline models. Across all models, 50-shot shows the largest improvement margin, compared to 5-shot and 10-shot. This is because with more shots, there are more samples to fine tune when performing fine tuning. In terms of DC, as we increase the number of shots not only do we have more few shot features, but we also have additional features sampled from the calibrated distribution leading to a better estimation of the ground truth distribution. DeepVoro Multi-label outperforms the individual models generalizing better on the query samples. This is because DeepVoro leverages diverse weak learners to make the ensemble better [6]. Our DeepVoro Multi-label model is enhanced with the presence of many overlapping labels closer in the feature space (multi-label NCA loss) and the use of additional support samples introduced by DC.

In Fig. 2, we select seven-class subset for the base classes to obtain a better projection of the image during training and five-class for the novel classes. The effective feature space sub-division of the component of our DeepVoro Multi-label, the *Backbone (FT) VD* model, is visualized by using the layer prior to the classification layer for extracting features. Three fully connected layers of sizes 512, 128, and 2 are added to generate a two-dimensional embedding of the high-dimensional data.

Table 2. AUC on five novel classes averaged over 100 episodes with 95% confidence intervals on MIMIC-CXR dataset. *Backbone (FT) classification* - using fully-connected classification layer. *FT* - Fine-tuned model with corresponding loss (BCE loss for *Backbone (FT) VD*, NCA loss for *NCA loss (FT) VD*) on support samples. *VD* - Voronoi diagram based soft nearest neighbor classification.

Model	5-shot	10-shot	50-shot
Backbone (FT) classification	0.611 ± 0.011	0.659 ± 0.009	0.706 ± 0.004
Backbone VD (Simpleshot) [21]	0.634 ± 0.012	0.668 ± 0.009	0.701 ± 0.004
Backbone (FT) VD	0.619 ± 0.013	0.670 ± 0.009	0.708 ± 0.004
NCA loss VD	0.614 ± 0.012	0.649 ± 0.008	0.680 ± 0.004
NCA loss (FT) VD	0.606 ± 0.014	0.636 ± 0.009	0.685 ± 0.005
DC (Voronoi-LR)	0.631 ± 0.011	0.653 ± 0.009	0.695 ± 0.004
DeepVoro Multi-label	**0.644 ± 0.012**	**0.679 ± 0.008**	**0.731 ± 0.004**

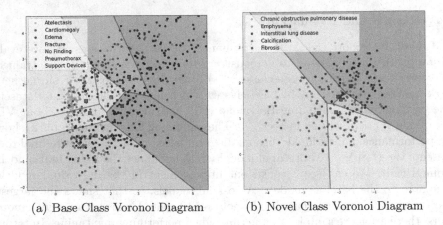

(a) Base Class Voronoi Diagram   (b) Novel Class Voronoi Diagram

Fig. 2. Feature space inducing a Voronoi diagram (VD). The VD of a subset of base classes (100 training and 100 test per class) and novel classes (5-way, 50-shot per class) in one episode in $\mathbb{R}^2$ respectively. Square boxes denote prototypes.

4   Conclusion

In this study, we show that our proposed method is able to effectively perform multi-label classification of less common chest X-rays using only a few samples. Our method proposes various schemes, including neighborhood component analysis loss, sampling from calibrated distributions, and fine-tuning using binary cross-entropy to adapt the residual neural network from base classes to novel classes in a multi-label setting. The resulting Voronoi diagrams from these methods are combined into our geometric DeepVoro Multi-label ensemble to achieve performance improvement over both simple fine-tuning and simpleshot baselines for identifying novel classes.

Acknowledgments. This material is based upon work supported by the National Library of Medicine under Award No. 4R00LM013001, and National Science Foundation under Grant No. 2145640 and No. 1910492.

References

1. Bendou, Y., et al.: Easy-ensemble augmented-shot-Y-shaped learning: state-of-the-art few-shot classification with simple components. J. Imaging **8**(7), 179 (2022)
2. Boots, B., Sugihara, K., Chiu, S.N., Okabe, A.: Spatial tessellations: concepts and applications of Voronoi diagrams (2009)
3. Chauhan, G., et al.: Joint modeling of chest radiographs and radiology reports for pulmonary edema assessment. In: Martel, A.L., et al. (eds.) MICCAI 2020. LNCS, vol. 12262, pp. 529–539. Springer, Cham (2020). https://doi.org/10.1007/978-3-030-59713-9_51

4. Chen, H., Miao, S., Xu, D., Hager, G.D., Harrison, A.P.: Deep hierarchical multi-label classification of chest X-ray images. In: Cardoso, M.J., et al. (eds.) Proceedings of the 2nd International Conference on Medical Imaging with Deep Learning. Proceedings of Machine Learning Research, 08–10 July 2019, vol. 102, pp. 109–120. PMLR (2019)
5. Dhillon, G.S., Chaudhari, P., Ravichandran, A., Soatto, S.: A baseline for few-shot image classification. In: International Conference on Learning Representations (2020)
6. Dvornik, N., Schmid, C., Mairal, J.: Diversity with cooperation: ensemble methods for few-shot classification. In: Proceedings of the IEEE/CVF International Conference on Computer Vision, pp. 3723–3731 (2019)
7. Finn, C., Abbeel, P., Levine, S.: Model-agnostic meta-learning for fast adaptation of deep networks. In: International Conference on Machine Learning, pp. 1126–1135. PMLR (2017)
8. Goldberger, J., Hinton, G.E., Roweis, S., Salakhutdinov, R.R.: Neighbourhood components analysis. In: Advances in Neural Information Processing Systems, vol. 17 (2004)
9. He, K., Zhang, X., Ren, S., Sun, J.: Deep residual learning for image recognition. In: Proceedings of the IEEE Conference on Computer Vision and Pattern Recognition (CVPR), June 2016
10. Ji, Z., Shaikh, M.A., Moukheiber, D., Srihari, S.N., Peng, Y., Gao, M.: Improving joint learning of chest X-ray and radiology report by word region alignment. In: Lian, C., Cao, X., Rekik, I., Xu, X., Yan, P. (eds.) MLMI 2021. LNCS, vol. 12966, pp. 110–119. Springer, Cham (2021). https://doi.org/10.1007/978-3-030-87589-3_12
11. Johnson, A.E., et al.: MIMIC-CXR, a de-identified publicly available database of chest radiographs with free-text reports. Sci. Data 6(1), 1–8 (2019)
12. Laenen, S., Bertinetto, L.: On episodes, prototypical networks, and few-shot learning. In: Advances in Neural Information Processing Systems, vol. 34, pp. 24581–24592 (2021)
13. Lakhani, P.: Deep convolutional neural networks for endotracheal tube position and X-ray image classification: challenges and opportunities. J. Digit. Imaging 30(4), 460–468 (2017)
14. Ma, C., Huang, Z., Gao, M., Xu, J.: Few-shot learning as cluster-induced Voronoi diagrams: a geometric approach. arXiv preprint arXiv:2202.02471 (2022)
15. Ma, C., Huang, Z., Gao, M., Xu, J.: Few-shot learning via dirichlet tessellation ensemble. In: International Conference on Learning Representations (2022)
16. Rajpurkar, P., et al.: CheXNet: radiologist-level pneumonia detection on chest X-rays with deep learning. arXiv preprint arXiv:1711.05225 (2017)
17. Seastedt, K.P., et al.: A scoping review of artificial intelligence applications in thoracic surgery. Eur. J. Cardiothorac. Surg. 61(2), 239–248 (2022)
18. Snell, J., Swersky, K., Zemel, R.: Prototypical networks for few-shot learning. In: Advances in Neural Information Processing Systems, vol. 30 (2017)
19. Tang, Y.X., et al.: Automated abnormality classification of chest radiographs using deep convolutional neural networks. NPJ Digit. Med. 3(1), 1–8 (2020)
20. Wang, S., Lin, M., Ding, Y., Shih, G., Lu, Z., Peng, Y.: Radiology text analysis system (RadText): architecture and evaluation. arXiv preprint arXiv:2204.09599 (2022)
21. Wang, Y., Chao, W.L., Weinberger, K.Q., van der Maaten, L.: SimpleShot: revisiting nearest-neighbor classification for few-shot learning. arXiv preprint arXiv:1911.04623 (2019)

22. Weng, W.H., Deaton, J., Natarajan, V., Elsayed, G.F., Liu, Y.: Addressing the real-world class imbalance problem in dermatology. In: Machine Learning for Health, pp. 415–429. PMLR (2020)
23. Yang, S., Liu, L., Xu, M.: Free lunch for few-shot learning: distribution calibration. In: International Conference on Learning Representations (2021)

Author Index

Printed in the United States
by Baker & Taylor Publisher Services